SEARCHING FOR
SASSY

SEARCHING FOR
SASSY

AN L.A. PHONE PSYCHIC'S TALES OF
LIFE, LUST & LOVE

Alyson Mead

BALBOA.
PRESS

A DIVISION OF HAY HOUSE

Balboa Press books may be ordered through booksellers or by contacting:

Balboa Press
A Division of Hay House
1663 Liberty Drive
Bloomington, IN 47403
www.balboapress.com
1-(877) 407-4847

ISBN: 978-1-4525-4194-5 (sc)
ISBN: 978-1-4525-4193-8 (hc)
ISBN: 978-1-4525-4195-2 (e)

Library of Congress Control Number: 2011919524

Printed in the United States of America

Balboa Press rev. date: 6/20/2011

"Space is big. Really big. You won't believe how hugely mindboggling big it really is."

—Douglas Adams,
The Hitchhiker's Guide to the Galaxy

For the freaks, the dark-humored,
and the slayers of ignorance.

Your weirdness will carry us forward.

July
✯ Cancer ✯

I am (re)born.

How did I get here? Who is responsible?

These are some, but not all, of the questions I ask myself as I park my stuff at a desk that defines nondescript, its beige prefab contours blending seamlessly into the slightly darker beige (yet fully carpeted) walls of my new home—a cubicle at AstralPlanet. I am just thirty, in full possession of my faculties, with an advanced degree from an ivy-beset eastern university. I am fit, attractive, vibrant and alive. A little hungry, but I noticed a taco truck on my way in. Maybe it will still be there when I get my first break.

What am I doing at a psychic line?

Long story.

New York City, my former home, had begun to close in like those spiky death walls in *Batman*, in the weeks following my breakup with Lonny. Five years is a long time to spend with someone so clearly not interested in a long-term future. But that's fodder for some future rant. Note to self: never again form or maintain a long-term relationship involving shared friends. In the all-too-real event of your demise as a couple, these poor souls will have to choose. And unless you want to spend all or most of

1

your time lobbying them for support, you will most likely be the one who loses out.

Speaking of walls closing in, I'm doing my best to listen as my new boss takes me through the rules of the job. His name is Martin. He's tall and dark, with feathered hair and a decidedly Baby Boomer attitude. He oozes enlightened masculinity in a Peter Coyote kind of way, touching my arm repeatedly as he illustrates how to operate the phones, how to transfer information to the call sheets we're given.

"Your phone will ring when one of the managers sends you a reading. You'll pick up, preferably on one ring, two at the most, and state your name."

I look at him doubtfully. The breakup has made me gun-shy, but he doesn't have to know that.

"You can make up a name, if you like. Lots of readers have a psychic name they use."

"OK."

"Anyway, you'll get their name and date of birth, which goes here . . . from that, you can tell if they're old enough to be on the call. If you get anyone younger than 18, tell them they have to get permission from a parent or guardian to have a reading."

I must be looking fuzzy, because he asks, "Am I going too fast?"

Not that it's beyond my comprehension. But all I can smell is incense, and hear the whirring of the copier right outside the door. The incense is something dark and cloying, and makes me a little swoony.

"No, I'm fine," I say.

"All right, then. The most important thing to remember is this: they'll have one question they want to ask. But your job is to keep them on the phone, so you'll want to ask them, 'What else can I answer for you today,' or 'Do you want me to look more deeply into that' . . . something along those lines."

"You want me to keep them on the phone?" *Oh silly girl.*

"You're being paid a base salary, per hour, but your salary includes an additional ten cents for every minute you can keep a caller on the line. There is a caveat, though."

"What's that?"

"As a rule, you don't want to go past twenty minutes, so keep an eye on the clock." Here, he indicates it, as if I'm a three-year old. Der, a clock.

"Twenty minutes," I say, noting it on a pad.

"We've found that if a reading goes over twenty minutes, people tend to complain to the phone company."

I smile weakly at him. Time has never been my strong suit.

He touches my arm again, soft as a rubber hammer, and gives me a smile. "You're going to be great," he says.

When he leaves the room, the phones start ringing again. A coincidence? I don't know yet.

Mercy is the manager on duty. A short blond with a wide-open corn-fed face, she radiates health and wellbeing. I know her already. She's how I got the job in the first place. Having spent the dough from a recent screenwriting assignment and finding myself with no real prospects, I spent my last twenty bucks on a tarot reading in an aromatherapy shop near a movie theater I attend frequently.

As the reader on duty, Mercy told me general but positive things about the future. But I have forgotten about the future. Los Angeles, which has seemed like sex and freedom covered with whipped cream and angels since my high school days spent worshipping the Doors, now feels spread-out and unfriendly.

I know just a few people after two months in town. And the city's strange beauty, seen on postcards and television screens the world over, seems hidden from my view. All I see are fancy cars, unhappy faces and strip malls. Ugly indeed.

Mercy is sunny today, a regular weather system unto herself. I wonder if she ever has rainy spells. "Hey, great to see you, Chica. You found your desk all right?"

"Yeah, it'll work."

She laughs. "It's usually pretty quiet in the afternoon," she says, "But later on, you'll probably get more readings. I'll just switch off with you and Katie. I'll do one, then give you three or four in a row. That way, you'll make more money."

She turns to a woman on my left, another blond, with dark streaks throughout. "Have you met Katie?"

"No," I say, turning to her.

Katie's a few years older than I am, with bright blue eyes and a guarded air.

"Hey, I'm Alyson." I stick out my hand; it's what I was taught to do.

She looks at my hand strangely, and then reaches for it. But not to shake, as I'm assuming. Instead, she turns my palm up to face her. "Look at that life line," she says, turning to Mercy. "Have you ever seen one like that? It goes clear over the Mound of Venus."

Mercy takes my hand, too, twisting and turning it in the low light.

"It's the Love Line that's broken. You'll have to tell us all about that . . ."

I try not to seem mortified. Is it that obvious, that I'm challenged in the Love Department? I imagine a bright red siren, beating out a tocsin from my heart.

The phone jangles, and I jump. I would say *saved by the bell*, but you knew that already.

Cancer, the 4th sign of the zodiac. The nurturer, the homebody, the mothering, sensitive one. I've been reading tarot cards for eight years now, since the summer after I graduated from college, but I need to brush up on my spotty knowledge of astrology. I'm sitting at my desk, waiting for my first actual call to come in:

> *Cancer in love can be a lovely thing, since this water sign wants to merge with others on a deep level. However, as the crab on the card's face attests, this sign can sometimes be too sensitive for its own good. The crab has a protective shell, and like this sea-going animal, Cancer natives may need to retreat from time to time to recuperate from intense emotional exchanges. Because you value love and family so much, you make a wonderful mate, providing a shoulder to cry on for your significant other when necessary, and creating a homey atmosphere around you.*

I think of New York, the sun-baked pavement on the day I left. I think of how tired I have been, trying to work 12-hour days, packing at night, worrying about money and the solo drive across the country. I think of the possessions given away, stuffed into dumpsters, left on the sidewalk—the slow dismantling of my old life. I think of the promise of this western city, its sparkling beaches and movie star homes. I think of the guy I left behind, issuing vague warnings of my inability to find anyone I'd love as much as him, and the one I thought there was a future with here. He, too, broke my heart, just days after I arrived. He's a Cancer.

I find a red pen in my bag and cross out what's written, adding my own opinion in the margin:

> *Cancer in love can be a ridiculous thing, since this water sign wants to stay away from anything scary and pretend it's all good in the 'hood with the old status quo. Though the Cancer native may want to feel deep, it's anything but, as it prefers personality deficits, fake tits and a complete lack of ambition to anything real. As the crab on this card's face attests, this sign can sometimes be so sensitive, it's fucking annoying. The crab has a protective shell, and you'll wish you had one, too, as this sign loves to break promises, dates and hearts like there's no tomorrow. Like the sea-going animal, Cancer natives may need to retreat from time to time, or maybe forever, from your life. Because they value love and family so much, they make wonderful mates for other people, not you! You provide endless opportunities for crying one's eyes out, and create a homey atmosphere around you, as long as home means an unending emotional hell.*

Juvenile? Yes.

Necessary? You bet.

All right, all right. A tad on the bitter side. *Whatever.*

It's my paperback, and I'll deface it if I want to.

I look around the room. A few psychics with their heads down, murmuring into their phones, reading, filing their nails, dreaming hard. Mercy's tilted back in her chair, staring at the ceiling tiles. When the phone rings, she picks it up without breaking her gaze, takes the information she needs and points to me.

I'm on.

Bronwyn is the psychic name I've come up with, a nod to my Welsh heritage. "AstralPlanet," I say into the receiver. "This is Bronwyn."

"I want to find out about . . ."

"Let me go ahead and get your name first."

"John."

"And your date of birth?"

"June 26ᵗʰ, 1972."

A Cancer. Of course.

"Great. What can I help you with today?"

"Like I said, I wanted to find out about my girlfriend."

I shuffle the cards and lay out a quick Celtic Cross. The missionary position of tarot. Quick, simple, not very original, but it gets the job done.

"It looks like you had a girlfriend, but she's not around anymore."

"Yeah."

An image forms in my mind. A gray cloud around him. Darkness on the walls, almost like his world is coated in motor oil. I can practically smell him. "She was looking for something else. Something you didn't have, or maybe didn't feel comfortable—"

"I got a job at Domino's, I told her. A good job . . . wait, I gotta put more money in."

I can hear the coins, a small universe of them, chunking against the metal of the payphone.

He doesn't wait until the noise subsides, so I only hear part of his next salvo. ". . . you gotta look like the New Kids on the

7

Block or something. Everyone's prejudiced against people who don't go to college, you know?"

I dart a glance to the clock. Just three minutes have passed. "Yeah," I murmur.

"I mean, it's like you get a better job or something if you go."

"Well, college does—"

"So my girlfriend's not coming back?"

"I don't see that, no."

"Bitch."

Remembering my training, I venture, "Do you want me to—"

"Another psychic told me something traumatic was going to happen to me. Is that true?"

I hate being interrupted. I *fucking hate* being interrupted. It's like this guy has found and pushed one of my biggest buttons without even trying.

I throw a few more cards down, and another image appears. A loss of virginity, of innocence. Somehow getting noticed for a weird talent he has. I see him writing a pamphlet with a unique perspective. Something military? No, it's a militia, with white supremacist elements. A doomsday prophecy, sketched out in a bunker.

Jesus.

"No, I don't see anything traumatic. You're going to be fine."

He hangs up the phone without a thank you. Seven and a half minutes has passed. I round it up to eight and update my sheet.

We all have to lose our cherries sometime.

The taco truck is indeed there when it's time for my break. I emerge into the blinding sunlight, low on the horizon. It bleeds orangey ooze everywhere as I squint to make sure my car is still parked where I left it, on the outskirts of the industrial park where AstralPlanet is located. The landscape is flatter than the plains here, and even the buildings seem to squat on the edge of something sandy colored and benign.

I order two chicken tacos that will hopefully respect my digestive tract. I have gotten used to eating street food in Manhattan, at lunchtime, coming home from clubs, and can't seem to find much of it in L.A. thus far. Hot dogs, knishes, hot pretzels and roasted chestnuts when it's freezing outside. I miss these things fiercely as I sit on the steps and try to open a Diet Pepsi with a broken pull-tab. I forgot they even made those anymore.

Finally, I stab it with a pen and it shoots like a geyser into the air. I water the plants in a trickling brown fountain. They look like they could use a drink.

I can smell the ocean when I get out of the car in Venice. Wanting to get as far away from New York as I could, I've taken a small apartment a block and a half away from the beach. If I walk down one block, I can see the place Jim Morrison used to live, now named after him, and I swear this was not by design. I didn't even know it was there when I rented my place—I just needed a place to live. But it feels somehow right and I am a little surer of my place in the world.

The manager of the apartment building is Rose, who's been around since the '60s. She tells me that the postman served in Vietnam and has flashbacks sometimes, forgets to deliver the mail and instead dumps it into the Pacific. More than once, she has comforted him with tea and more, before sending him back out on his rounds. She has told me not to go down by the beach at night, that homeless guys, some of them violent and withdrawing from meds, will knock me on my white ass to steal anything they can sell or trade for drugs.

Though I'm in the mood for some romantic ocean viewing, I'm inclined to follow her advice for now. So I check the mail (nothing there today—should I be happy or worried?) and head upstairs. Fish, a guy from a popular local band, lived in my apartment before me, gifting me with a drawer full of tools, nails and fuses before he left. He's also left behind an enormous graphic painting on my door, which I've refused to have painted over in his honor, though Rose was kind enough to offer.

I let myself in, nodding to my neighbor across the way, and plop down on the uncomfortable-as-shit futon I bought at Ikea a week or so ago. It's big enough for two average sized people sitting side by side, or three if they have very small asses. My apartment is barely decorated—just a few postcards picked up from my cross-country road trip tacked up over my computer, and I still have to determine how to handle the kitchen area, part of the living room, really, which is delineated with a foot or two of press-on vinyl tile butting up against the indoor-outdoor carpeting.

I hate television, and have yet to hook up my VCR, so I assail my boom box with a mix tape given to me by a friend for the trip—a mix of punk rock, psychobilly and old classics keeps me company as I do the dishes. For someone who doesn't eat a lot, and not very much at home, I can accumulate some serious dish build-up.

Something about the repetitive motion of hands on dish, the soapy water, the smells rising to my nostrils, makes me think about New York again. Maybe it's because I haven't been gone long enough, or been here long enough, to have any real sense of where I belong. I didn't have mixed feelings about moving here when I left. I knew what I wanted, and moved toward it, even if it scared the crap out of me.

I'm here, I think, now what?

The phone rings, the way it does in movies, not my real life. I reach for it without drying my hands, daring electricity to shock me.

It's my friend Felicity, who's known me since we both lived in New York, and has been in L.A. for three or four years now.

She is breathless with excitement. "I met this guy at the dog park. And he's perfect for you."

Felicity takes care of animals, walks dogs and manages to act in a few movies, TV shows and commercials every year. No mean feat. The dog park is like her second home.

I am doubtful. "What's he like?' I ask.

"Tall, dark. He's into music . . . just the way you like them."

I have a love-hate relationship with guys in bands. I love them for awhile, and then I usually hate them. "I may be swearing off musicians."

"You're a liar," she says, laughing. "The last guy you went out with was in that band—what was it called?"

Low blow, Lady. *Low blow.*

"Bad Girls Get Dates. BGGD."

"I *love* that name."

"Go ahead, get your laughs in. You'll be sorry when I'm in a nunnery."

"You have to meet him." How she talks me into it, I'll never know. But I am giving her permission to release my digits to him shortly thereafter.

We hang up and a dripping noise makes me look down. A decent sized puddle of water and dish soap is pooled next to my foot. Fuck. I don't own a mop. There goes another improvised dishtowel, and one more thing to wash.

Grocery shopping used to be one of my least favorite things to do. In the East Village, you had three choices: shop at an overpriced Korean grocer, a scary bodega (ants in your Pop-Tarts, anyone?), or frequent Key Foods on Avenue A. Key Foods bore some resemblance to the grocery stores I had been to as child on eastern Long Island, with actual produce, canned goods, a cereal aisle and the like. But unless you liked lying on the floor trying to help an elderly lady corner the market on chunk light tuna from the bottom shelf (this happened; it was on sale), or dodging slobbering junkies looking for the sugariest snacks known to humankind, Key Foods was not what you'd call fun, even if it was open 24 hours a day.

In California, grocery shopping is like paradise after being confined on a Russian gulag. The produce is hallucinatory, it's so vibrant, and you start to wonder if you've ever seen an apple before, or a lemon. Honeydews assume a kind of super-sensual capacity. They just seem so . . . knowing. Cantaloupes are wise, strawberries like whispering friends trying to make your life happier just by being. Whatever they're planning, they have your best interests at heart.

I have been an insomniac for most of my life, made worse by my terrible diet soda habit. And maybe it's the time difference, and my lack of inner adjustment. Maybe it's my shifts, which can start at 6:00 AM, 5:00 PM or noon, but I find myself pulling into Lucky's parking lot between 1 and 2 AM. Whenever the urge to shops comes upon me, it's usually around then.

If you've never been shopping for groceries at that hour, I strongly urge you try it, at least once. You get an entirely different crowd from the people shopping during the day, and even if you need to stay a bit more alert than normal, you'll reap a lifetime of stories. When I enter the store that night, there is a woman at the check stand, arguing with a dark-haired woman about her fistful of coupons, apparently all expired, not by days or weeks, but by years.

"Ma'am, listen to me," she says, in heavily accented English. "We don't even sell these products anymore."

"But I need them!" She seems desperate. The checker darts a glance to the security guard, who stands by, disinterested.

She tries again, another tack. "I can't even scan these. They won't go through the machine, because they have a different code. *Entiende?*"

"I want to see the manager," the woman demands.

The checker allows herself a brief moment of relief as she moves to the cage, where two men hunch over receipts.

I push my cart, grabbing items without much thought. I am only half here for the food. The other half shamelessly eavesdrops on personal conversations about pregnancy tests and which kind of condom to buy. I learn how much fiber a woman believes her husband needs for his diet, and what foods little Jimmy will and won't eat. By the end of my excursion, I know a lot.

The produce I always save for last. After eight years in New York, you learn to appreciate produce. What passes for decent fruit and vegetable matter, in stores at least, has been desiccated past the point of nutrition. It wilts there, sadly, begging you with its little self to put it out of its misery, which you would do, being a kindly sort, if you had knives that sharp, or a big mallet of some kind. So mostly you pass the produce by and wait for the Farmer's Market.

Tonight, the apples are gleaming in five colors, like spectral magisters. There is a guy whose job it is to water the produce, endlessly spritzing them with a misting hose. He seems proud of his work, and polishes the apples individually. I see him doing this at night because there are fewer people in the store. He works silently, using a special towel, not displaying them for the love of the shoppers or even his boss, but seemingly for the apples themselves. I like him, though all we've ever done is nod to one another as I choose some carrots, a head of broccoli and usually a pear or two.

The coupon woman is gone when I approach the checker, who looks like she'd rather eat a live rat than wait on me. I pile my stuff on the belt and push it toward her. She passes it over the scanner, frowning slightly when the clam chowder's price won't appear on her monitor.

"Do you know how much this is?" she asks.

"Sorry, no," I say, feeling guilty somehow for not noticing.

But she shouts a stream of Spanish into a microphone. Her voice is amplified overhead, and a similarly rapid volley of Spanish tells her what she needs to know. My purchase complete, I make my way to my tiny, brave car, veteran of the I-9 and the 78, the 40 and 210.

I'm loading the bags into the backseat when an elderly man approaches, wearing a smile that has long since died on his face. "You been to Mardi Gras?" he asks.

"Pardon?"

He points inside, where bright colored beads are wound around the rearview mirror.

"Oh, yeah. I went to Mardi Gras a few years ago." The memory seems caught in my brain, refusing to come forward now.

"Been there myself, back in the '60s."

"Yeah?"

"Seen some wild things there, too." I notice his accent sounds Midwestern, flat around the consonants. Not from around here, like me.

I wonder what brought him here. Love, money, or both?

"Been on the Rex float, throwin' them beads at the ladies." His face relaxes, far away. "Green, purple and gold. Those were the colors. Still got some of the money, too."

"Sounds like you had a good time." I close the door and move to the driver's side, trying not to be rude.

"Yup, I did at that. Have a good night, Miss." He goes into the store, pausing just once, to wave back at me. "'One of the best times in my life," he murmurs.

People who aren't in relationships can do these things, because there's no one at home waiting for them. I am one of the unclaimed, the detritus, the alone. I am one of them.

I feel sadder than a dirge as I pull out of the parking lot and drive home.

The next morning I rise, after little sleep. Six AM shifts are good for two things. The first is that they get me, a night person if ever there was one, out of bed. The second is traffic. There is little of it as I swing into the closest thing I can find to a deli in Venice and amble in for a couple of Diet Dr. Peppers. Ammunition for the day. People wander around with their heads down, sunglasses covering hangovers and surgery healings.

Today I have a new manager. Radar is a tall man, at least six four in stocking feet, with ursine gentleness. We shake hands when I walk in with my diet ammo and velvet clad cards. But then he goes back to reading the newspaper, creasing it carefully when he turns a page.

I tuck into *Memories, Dreams, Reflections* and wonder what Jung would make of last night's dream. I was saying goodbye to my lover at the airport. Though I couldn't tell what city we were in, or who he was, I tried to be brave. The mask didn't last, though, and I started to cry a little. He hugged me to his chest, thinking I didn't care about him that much, and my face fell to my chest in embarrassment. He lifted my face up to his and kissed me. His face was filled with love and compassion. Who the hell is this guy?

I feel myself being split open, and stuff flies out, flapping around the airport like wounded butterflies. It leaves my body in ribbons, like a magician's trick gone wrong, racing for the skylight, crashing there and falling back down to earth. I can see hands sweeping the dead butterflies over a cliff that has appeared at the edge of the airport. A broom appears. When the sun comes up, it bathes me in a bright purple light.

Radar answers a call, takes down some information, then passes the call off to me.

"Hi, it's Bronwyn, can I get your name, please?"

"Carol."

"And your date of birth?"

"July 18th, 1951."

"Excellent, thanks. How can I help you today?"

"Well, I have to tell you that I'm a psychoanalyst, and don't really believe in this."

"OK."

"I'm also a model, actress and mortician."

Did she just say mortician?

"All right."

"I hope you don't mind but I'm calling you from the bathtub. I'm having a glass of champagne because I'm exhausted."

I laugh while I bang the cards together, mixing them up. "It's okay with me. What did you want to ask about?"

"I had this man . . . well, he was my boyfriend, but we broke up a few days ago."

"Do you want to see about getting back together with him?"

I hear splashing sounds.

"Yes," she finally says, like she knows it's the wrong question to ask.

I lay out the cards. "You're better off without him," I say. "Does he drink?"

"Yeah."

"Did he hit you?"

"Sometimes."

"It doesn't look like he was working, either."

"No."

"Why not?"

"We were buying this place together, then he decided to quit his job." Curious logic.

"Why?"

"I don't know."

"You didn't talk about it? He just did it?"

"Yeah."

"I really think you're better off without him."

Carol shifts in the water quietly. I hear her sip from the glass. "So, there's no chance of getting back together with him?"

"There's another woman he's seeing."

Sighing, she answers, "Yeah, he cheated on me all the time."

"Honey . . ." I feel an odd compassion for Carol.

"I know. I'm better off without him. It's just that I put a lot of work into him."

"And a lot of money, it looks like."

"Yeah, I paid for him to go into treatment. He was addicted to drugs."

"Oh." Nothing else to say to that.

"And, well, it was hard to get his trust."

"Yeah?"

"Yeah. You see, his wife died. She was killed in a car crash."

"God, that's terrible."

"Yeah. And the thing was that when they found her, she was with four men."

"In the car?"

I visualize this woman as a member of a bowling team, making her weekly trip to the lanes in a car pool.

Carol goes on. "Yeah. When the cops got there, all of them were naked."

I swallow and speak carefully. "All five of them?" This was a bowling team I had to check out sometime.

"Yeah, they all died."

Nervously, I play with the cards—Two of Swords, Page of Pentacles, Strength—a crossroads, and the courage required to move through it. "I'm sorry about that. Did you have any other questions tonight?"

"No, thanks. I'd better go now." Carol splashes once more and hangs up.

Twelve minutes. I mark the call sheet and ask Radar for a bathroom break. Outside, staring at the sky, I wonder what Gods

I've offended in some previous incarnation. What I've done to land me in this place.

That night, I receive a call from Ron, the guy Felicity's convinced will make me forget all about New York and its masculine gifts. I like his voice right away, because he sounds like he's been around the block a few times, and maybe did a stint as a late-night DJ at some point.

He's in a band. Of course.

"I hear you're just here from New York. I used to live there."

"Really?"

"Yeah, my wife and I lived in Brooklyn for a bit, then the Lower East Side."

Well, at least he's capable of committing.

"Ahh, my old 'hood."

Two hours later, we're still talking. We've covered everything from Carl Jung to mythology and my new job as a psychic. I don't even consider myself that. I can read cards, that much I know. But weirdly, he seems impressed. Maybe he thinks I'll tell him something deep, though that's not likely.

I realize we have a lot in common, and even though I've sworn off men, maybe not forever, but until my heart grows back, he seems like a nice enough guy. We make plans to meet at the Beverly Hills Library, where I'm researching a project I'd like to write someday.

If the date sucks, I can always go back to the books, which seldom disappoint.

After I hang up, I realize I may be having company soon, so I pick up the junk on the floor—newspapers I haven't figured out how to recycle yet, magazines, notes and books, some discarded clothing and a Necco Wafer wrapper, the spoils of my cross-country trip come to an end.

I wonder what the Cancer's doing, living not more than two miles from here. Is he thinking of me, or happily engaged in some form of domestic bliss? Should I even waste my time thinking about him, what might have been? Probably not.

I sit on the floor, without a couch or chair yet. At least my domain is clean, relatively clean.

In the other room is a suitcase, open on the floor, and a futon. Sexy.

This is stupid. It's got to change. He's made his choice, and I am not it.

I can't quite muster a "his loss," but I get up, renewed, determined. There has to be a way to fix up this place with very little money, get a home vibe going somehow. I cut some stars out of aluminum foil and form them into a constellation on the upper part of the wall, winding a strand of Christmas lights along them. There. Cheerier, definitely.

There's a bottle of champagne in the refrigerator, something I thought I'd share with someone. But now is the moment, and this is the place. Paper cups, a toast to my new place.

This is home now. Make the best of it, girl.

The next day is hotter than I'm used to, sunnier than shit and beating into my brain as I get out of my car and scuttle towards the library entrance as if I'll burst into flame at any moment. I recognize the parking gate and the speaker Eddie Murphy spoke into in *Beverly Hills Cop*, I think. Even the police look like film extras here, and I watch them behind my shades as they lounge against their bikes, which have never seen the grit of the freeway.

Ron is leaning against the wall close to the whooshing entrance, looking cool. I walk toward him, taking him in. Brown hair, longer than I usually go for, but he's tall and built.

He takes off his sunglasses as I move closer.

"Alyson?" he asks.

"Yeah, it's me."

His eyes move over me. I can feel the electricity there. No mistaking it.

"The red hair gave you away."

I laugh.

"No, really, it's hot. You look great."

All right, he's pretty cute. I'll give this a shot, and see where it goes.

August
✮ Leo ✮

I am confused.

The next morning, all of the psychics are called into AstralPlanet for some sort of meeting. We shuffle in, regardless of shift times. I'm too new to be afraid of the line closing down or laying people off but a few of the psychics, people I've never met before, whisper to one another as we go into the conference room.

"If they lay us off, I'm going to fucking Sedona. I'm sick of this shit."

"I hear you, sister."

The conference room is as generic as they come, with gray carpeting, fake brown paneling from the Office Depot School of Decorating, and an oblong table that looks like it may be made of particle board under the thick chocolate varnish coating. I'm afraid to put my elbows on it, resting my hands in my lap instead. Mercy and Katie come in, and take seats on either side of me.

Martin comes in, frowning at a clipboard. People quiet down as he takes his seat.

"I've been going over the average hold times, and they're down almost twenty percent from last quarter. We're going to have to pick that up."

Emma, a woman who works off-site, speaks up, "I get so many fuck you calls, it's hard to do that."

"Fuck you calls?"

"Yeah, as soon as you answer the phone, they scream 'fuck you' into the phone and hang up."

Martin looks to Mercy, who's practically swooning. I'm noticing now that there's some energy there, but I can't tell if it's happened yet, or if she just wants it to happen. She nods to him, confirming the rumor.

"Well, we can work to screen those calls a little better, but we have to improve at asking for the next question. You could even move to it, without asking."

"That doesn't sound ethical." Radar is the only one who could probably get away with that, since he's about the same age as Martin, and several inches taller.

"I'm not asking you to hurt anyone. We just need to establish ourselves as the best service of this kind."

I look around at Radar again, and don't have to wonder what he's thinking. He looks down at a notebook he always carries, and scribbles away at a drawing I can't see. He thinks it's pure bullshit.

"Anyone have any questions?"

Martin looks around the table, but most of the psychics are afraid of losing their jobs, so much so that they don't want to rock the boat.

Satisfied, he says, "Great. I want to do a group meditation before you go. So everyone please close your eyes and just let yourself relax."

I close my eyes, keeping my hands in my lap.

"Uncross your legs, your ankles, your arms, your hands . . ."

Whoops. I uncross.

"Then picture a rose. This rose begins as a bud. It's bright, brilliant red, tightly closed."

Breathing in, breathing out. A rose in my mind.

"See the rose beginning to open, as if the sun's shining on it. As the rose opens, see it getting bigger and bigger. See the petals opening and you can smell the rose now. It's filling your nostrils with its sweet, sweet scent."

The rose in my mind grows bigger. I can smell it, close as if it were in the room. But my imagination has always been this suggestive, for better or worse.

"As the rose seems like it's going to get bigger than you can possibly hold in your mind, bigger than you are, or the room, or even the building, see it exploding."

Huh? I open one eye cautiously and catch Katie's eye. She gives me a wry smile. Seen it all before.

"Explode the rose and see its petals raining over everything. See them raining over Los Angeles, getting caught in the trees, being wiped away by passing cars, going down the chimneys in Beverly Hills, falling into the ocean."

For some reason, my mind has stuck in that position, with the rose half-exploded. Maybe I need some WD-40 or something. I pretend to keep going.

"When your rose is completely exploded, open your eyes."

I do, looking around to find my co-workers doing the same. Only they don't look confused and slightly creeped out. I don't dare look at Katie. I'm sure to crack up inappropriately.

Martin is standing at the head of the table, looking vaguely royal. Or maybe that's what he wants us to see. "The rose is our business, and we're going to explode it together."

Still having a hard time with the analogy, but I don't dare let on. I like having food. Paying rent. Buying gas for my car.

Mercy raises her hand and Martin acknowledges her. "I just want to say that I got a lot out of that," she says. "Really excellent visualization."

He considers this for a few seconds, not deigning to give her a smile of appreciation. "Well, we're not doing it for commentary, but thanks just the same."

She just smiles to herself, not seeming to notice the diss.

We're all dismissed, and I go downstairs to start my shift.

A few minutes later, I am signed on and get my first call. He's a Scorpio trying to manifest his soulmate.

"I've tried the personals, but can't seem to meet anyone."

"Let me look into that for you." I lay down the Two of Cups, the Two of Swords and the Page of Wands—someone out there for him, definitely. A picture of her begins to form in my mind: a petite brunette with olive skin and a pretty smile.

"I can see that you're doing a lot, but I have to say it's not that. Your effort is in the wrong area."

"What do you mean?"

"The effort isn't external, it's internal."

"You mean I have to be ready for her?"

"Kind of. But it's more that you need to believe in your own power. You know all about manifesting. You know you need to do it, and even how to do it. Now you have to convince yourself that you *can* do it. Does that make sense?"

"I think so."

"You have a great deal of power, and I can see that there's someone waiting on the periphery of your life. Someone you know knows her, and all you have to do is be available."

He laughs. "I'm definitely that."

"I can see a choice you have to make about yourself. And once you've done that, she'll come in very naturally."

"I hope you're right."

"I can just tell you what I see, but I hope it works out for you."

"Thanks."

"Can I answer anything else for you today?"

"No, thank you. What's your name again?"

"Al—I mean, Bronwyn."

"I'll ask for you next time, Bronwyn."

I'm a big deal in the psychic world, at least for the next few minutes of my life.

The afternoon is slow, and I daydream about my date with Ron yesterday. It's been some time since I was on the back of a motorcycle, and he has to tell me not to lean into the turns as we wind our way into the Hollywood Hills and an overlook he knows about. We walk around a gorgeous overhung garden so green that my senses go into overdrive. The closest thing New Yorkers have to this is the Botanical Garden all the way up in the Bronx, which was way too far for a downtown girl. Bright bougainvillea burst open in fuchsia and tangerine, twisting their vines across the path.

We sit at a picnic table and talk, and I am shy and awkward, realizing I've never really dated before, or had to. I don't understand the first thing about it. All I know is who I vibe with and who I don't. And I am definitely vibing with this guy now.

"Felicity said you were into filmmaking."

"Yeah, I went to film school briefly," I say, laughing nervously, "and then I made a film she was in right before I got kicked out."

Open mouth, insert foot.

He gives me a conciliatory look, and I stagger on.

"It's no big deal, well at the time it was, I guess, but now I'm over it. I made my movie, which went to festivals and got a modest distribution deal, and then I made a TV pilot and a few music videos."

"Wow, that's really cool."

"They're all really small, I mean micro-budgets, really. No one's heard of them at all, unless they happen to be related to me."

What the hell is wrong with me?

He laughs. Nice, trying to bail me out. "You're in for a surprise. Most people in Los Angeles are completely different from you. They think they invented the motion picture business by themselves, and have no trouble telling you that."

I hang my head a little, making an embarrassed face. "Maybe my schtick could use some work."

"Or maybe not. You want to come over for dinner?"

"Sure."

The ride back down from the Hills isn't bad, either, as the sun flits through the trees. The sleepy sunlit feeling I remember from album covers, dreaming in my room, is real now. It's part of my real life. I'm riding on the back of a motorcycle like any average California chick, red hair blowing out behind me, clutching onto his midsection and wondering what's underneath.

He makes me fresh pasta (really!), and lets me help stuff the little packages with a spinach and garlic mixture while his miniature bulldog capers around my feet. Pets are another novelty, since New York apartments, not to mention our overly long hours spent trying to pay for same, prevent us from exploring much beyond cats (very allergic, no thanks), birds (too scary and loud) and lizards (tried that, left him with my ex).

The dog is sweet though a tad crazy, tearing from room to room with a chew toy now, then a couch pillow and finally a pair of Ron's underwear from the other room. He grabs them, stuffs them into a kitchen cabinet, and banishes her to the living room. Obediently, she droops off, lying on an area rug in his sightline and hanging her head.

The food is delicious and I can't believe after so many years of eating out, or cooking for other people (Lonny and his bandmates, most of the time), someone's making me food I have no idea how to conceive, no less make. It's heaven, and I have to refrain from gobbling.

Afterwards, he pours me a glass of wine and rubs the back of my neck with his thumb. Oh God, my spot. He found it on the first try. Bastard.

Then we're kissing and disrobing, and the fumbling trip to the bedroom is spent trying to keep our lips locked together. The small space of this room, the light spilling in from outside. His hands wise and sure on my waist . . .

The phone jangles me out of the daydream. I'm back on.

"Is this the psychic?"

"Yes, my name is Bronwyn, and I just have to get some information from you before we get started. Your name and date of birth, please?"

"I just told the other lady."

"It's just so I know how to refer to you. And I use the birth date to help read you."

"No, I want to talk to a psychic. A real psychic."

Though I still don't believe it myself, I tell her, "Psychics use tarot cards to help them focus."

"Don't you have any real psychics there?"

"I'm not sure what you mean . . ."

She exhales at the sheer inconvenience of it all. "All right, then, my name is Jennifer and my birthday is June 17, 1981."

So young to be such a bitch.

"All right, Jennifer, did you want to ask a question, or have me give you a general reading?"

"I want to ask about this guy I've been seeing."

"What's his name?"

"You don't know?"

I assume she's joking, but soon realize she's not. "I want to make sure I'm reading the right person."

Another exhalation. "George."

"Well, I'm getting three months . . ."

"Yeah, we've been seeing each other for three months."

"I can see that you want to get serious . . ."

"Yeah, that's my question. I want to know if we're going to get married."

I shuffle the cards and lay them in a quick Celtic Cross. Kings in three suits, the Four of Wands . . . whoa, and the Ten of Swords.

"I can see that someone's been having trouble staying faithful," I say, hoping to strike a diplomatic tone. Half expecting the phone to slam down in my ear, I lay down another card—the Moon—confusion and deceit.

"Yeah, I saw this other guy for awhile . . . just a few times. It was just sex."

"I'm not seeing that you're very close to George, though. Are you still together?"

"Kind of . . ."

"But you want to marry him."

"Yeah." *Is she chewing gum, or is that some sort of nervous tic?*

"I'm not sure why you cheated on him, then."

"Because he's a dick!" She bangs the phone down in my ear.

Twelve minutes. Not a bad hold time, even for someone who's admittedly still learning the ways of the heart.

Katie comes in a few minutes later and logs in with Mercy, the afternoon manager. Maybe it's my influence, but she's carrying an armload of library books.

"Hey you," she says, nodding in my direction. "Explode any roses lately?"

I dart a glace to Mercy and stifle a laugh.

"I'll talk to you later," she promises.

Sure as Big friggin' Ben, Mercy takes a smoke break at the top of the hour, forwarding the phones first to Katie, then to me.

She's barely out the door when Katie wheels her office chair over and whispers, "She so wants Martin, it's not even funny."

"I thought I noticed something going on there."

"She'd do him on the conference table if he asked."

I ask, "So what was the deal with the exploding rose?"

Katie exhales. "I have no fucking idea. He's always coming up with these retarded little things. Maybe he thinks they're 'spiritual.'" She makes little quote marks in the air with her fingers. "Saturn in Leo. He's a natural born performer, but there's this part of him that doesn't want to admit that he likes attention."

I give her a look.

"What, you thought you were working in a normal place?" she giggles. "These people are insane, I'm telling you."

"How long have you been here?"

"Around a year, but most of us came over when the last line went out of business."

It doesn't cross my mind to ask if this happens on a regular basis. I am happy to have any means of support, no matter how pathetic.

Katie leans over towards my desk, piled with a few books and a notebook. I have no idea how busy my shifts will be yet, so I tend to come over-prepared. "What are you reading?" she asks.

I hold up the Jung book, almost finished now.

"Do you know you're the only person who reads here?"

I hadn't noticed yet. "Really? What do they do?"

"Nothing, mostly. Wilma watches *Star Trek* . . ."

"Wilma?"

Katie rolls her eyes. "You'll meet her. She thinks she's an alien."

Huh?

"I told you, they're all crazy."

Her phone rings, and she turns to answer it, circling her temple with an index finger.

I relax into my book again, pausing to take notes as they come up. Mercy walks back in from her smoke break, trailing an obnoxious chemical trail and takes her seat a few seconds before Martin walks in.

Katie hangs up her call, tallies her hold time and updates her sheet before turning to him. "Hi handsome," she coos, "have you come to visit me?"

His reaction is curious. A crooked eyebrow, a la Spock, a nervous smile. He's clearly turned on, but before he can answer, Mercy flutters over with something or other. Office politics, psychic style. I have no idea what everyone wants here.

I thought Katie was married. At least she's wearing a lapis ring on that finger.

Mercy's trying to block Katie with her body, like some sort of adolescent. Amateur hour, he's clearly not interested. I go back to my book.

"Nice hold times," I hear, over my left shoulder. Martin's standing there, looming over me.

He points to the single two-minute call on the sheet and asks, "What about this one?"

"That was a fuck-you call." They're common enough. Teenagers grabbing handfuls of power wherever they can. He stands there for a few more seconds until I finally go back to reading.

"You sure do read a lot," he says.

I bury my face deeper in the pages.

"That book must be pretty interesting."

I have no idea how to answer that. He tries again, "So, you're reading Jung?"

"Yes." Slowly, I tilt my face up to appraise him.

"I studied at the Jungian Institute."

"In Switzerland?"

"No, here in L.A."

"Oh."

Reading is the one perk of the job, and I aim to enjoy every minute of it between calls. My eyes return to the book. I can feel his eyes to my shoulder where, I realize, one bra strap is showing. Using my peripheral vision, I subtly extend my fingers to bury it under the edge of my tee shirt.

"I think Emma Jung's involvement was very interesting in the context of her husband's career."

"In what sense?" My interest is piqued. Perhaps Martin actually has a few thoughts rattling around in there.

"Well, she was an analyst herself. But she gave all that up when Carl started to have the affair with Toni."

"Well, not completely. It's not like she stood around all day in the kitchen stirring soup or something."

"She gave up her career so he could explore his anima with his mistress."

"You think that's noble?"

"Well, he was the more gifted analyst."

"I think it's a shame that one person has to be subverted in order for the couple to survive."

Martin just stares at me coldly, as if he were about to apply a knife to the bottom of my soft abdomen, slice up and dissect me. "You're still young, but you'll see. Everything has to add up. It's all got to balance. You have to do the math, like when you balance your checkbook."

"I prefer credit," I snap.

He walks out of the room. Angrily, I bite my challenging tongue. I face my phone and will it to ring.

A few seconds later, it does. I try to make my voice sound bright and cheerful. "What can I help you with today?"

The caller's voice is devoid of energy. "I don't really know. All I can think about is killing myself."

"I can read you if you'd prefer, but I have an 800 number if you feel you'd rather speak with someone who can help you. It's free." They've given us this list in case of emergencies. I'm not experienced enough yet to tell if this is one or not.

"No, you'll do."

Way to make a girl feel wanted, dude.

33

"Do you see my life getting better anytime soon? Is it even worth it to go on?"

I shuffle the cards. This is going to be a long day.

Luckily, it turns out that another dose of anti-depressants will do just the trick, and all I can hope is that the guy calls his doctor soon. I can't do much more than that.

On the way home from work, I stop at a furniture rental store on Lincoln. All my possessions fit into a Volkswagen Fox, so I've been doing without a real bed, table or dresser for several weeks now. Makes life simple if you're short, which I'm not. I can do without all the bending; my back has begun to ache.

I've never heard of renting your furniture before. In New York, I managed to have a bed, hand-painted dresser, futon couch and a desk. But here, there are so many transients that these smart people are filling a needed niche. Why bother to buy places to sit, places to sleep, if you may not achieve your dream this year, or ever?

After browsing around the showroom for a bit, I choose the least offensive wooden furniture I can find, a dresser and bed, as well as a lamp (I've forgotten that little detail as well, and not every room in my apartment has overhead lights) before speaking with a sales rep. He looks like he hawks cars in his spare time, straight out of Central Casting. A cheap suit, slicked down hair, a few bitten pens in his jacket pocket.

"It's gonna be a $320 payment when it's delivered," he says. "That includes the $200 deposit, which is refundable when you cancel your contract, and the $120 monthly fee."

"Do you take checks?" I haven't gotten around to getting a credit card yet, and don't want to do too much damage to my mom's.

He brushes his hair back with one practiced palm, though it would be impossible for any of his hairs to actually move. "Absolutely. Now let's see about a delivery time."

My new life is completely beige, to match my job. Nice.

Ron calls when I get in, just when I'm beginning to think I've made a mistake by sleeping with him on the first date. I've never been one to draw out the inevitable to absurd proportions. If I like someone, I'm not very good at waiting. I'm OK with that.

"Hey," he purrs. "I've been thinking about you."

"Yeah?" I'm trying to cut up some mushrooms and red peppers without dropping the phone.

"I was wondering what you're doing tomorrow night. I'm going to be in Santa Monica and could stop by your place."

Yikes. The furniture isn't due to be delivered until three days from now.

"That's possible," I say. "But I have to be honest. I have very little furniture, and there's barely anyplace to sit . . ."

"I'm not coming for the furniture, babe."

Which is the right thing to say, of course.

"All right then. What do you want to do?"

"What do *you* want to do?"

He's giving me all kinds of evil ideas, but I'll have to settle for the obvious. "Well, since you made me dinner, I could do the same for you."

"Sounds like a plan. I'll be there around 7:00, if that's good."

"That's good."

"Can't wait . . ." He hangs up, leaving me horny and unfulfilled.

My stomach growls. I'm back to the vegetables, though all I want is boy.

I'm lying on the floor reading when Felicity calls, a few hours later. Dinner was unsatisfactory, masturbation only makes me more frustrated, and I can tell from the sound of her voice that all is not well. Felicity is one of the few married friends I have, and I kind of look up to that because it seems so much more mature than I'm capable of being, at this point, anyway. I've never given marriage much thought, except when Lonny said he would marry me so we could get all the money and presents, as long as we got divorced the following week. Asshole.

"What's up?" I ask. "You sound . . . weird."

"Can I come and stay with you for awhile?"

"Sure, what's going on?"

"Well, we're having some problems, and I need a place to go."

"You know I don't have the most comfortable accommodations, but you're welcome."

"Good, because I'm around the corner. Can I come over now?"

This only happens to single friends, I surmise. We exist in married people's lives to be their anchors, when their shit gets all kinds of lost.

"Absolutely. Can you bring some beer?"

We spend the next few hours talking about life, and marriage, and her husband Freddie, who she's only been married to for maybe two years, tops. I don't know what makes people want to cheat. It's happened to me before, and I suppose I've done it to someone else once. But that was out of revenge, and I don't know if it counts, or should count as much.

Her normally lovely face is stricken and drawn, and her blond ringlets seem matted down, especially at the back of her head, like she's been sleeping in her car. I don't ask.

"I don't know how it happened. I just met this guy, you've probably met him too, at one of our parties. He's tall, brown eyes . . . anyway, I just went over there to run lines with him for this short film we're doing together, and . . ."

I'm not sure I want to hear this. It's my only relatively healthy version of marriage, with my parents, and most everyone else's parents around me, long separated or divorced.

". . . he just came up to me, and it was like I was hypnotized. He was kissing me, and kind of grabbing me . . . and then he was on top of me, and my clothes were coming off."

I know I don't want to hear this, but I want to be there for my friend.

"Did you guys do it?" I feel like a teenager. I haven't used the phrase "do it" in about a hundred years. But it seems fitting right now, though unintentionally delicate. She doesn't blink.

"Yeah . . . well, no. He was on top of me and then he just kind of pulled it out and jerked off on me."

"*On* you?"

"Yeah."

"I feel like an asshole, and I shouldn't have told Freddie, but I did, and now he's not talking to me."

I crack open another beer and hand it to her. "I'm sorry. But I think he'll talk to you again in a few days, or maybe even a few hours, who knows?"

"You don't mind that I'm staying here?"

"As long as you make yourself scarce when Ron comes over," I say, only half joking.

Felicity makes her mouth into a surprised O. "How's that going?"

"All right." I can tell I'm blushing, and graze my eyes across the floor.

"You whore!" she says. "You slept with him."

"Maybe."

Felicity laughs, and it's worth it, to see that scared and mortified look wiped off her face. She is young again for an instant, and so am I.

I have a roommate for the next few days, as we get used to our very different schedules in a small space together. My shifts happen at 6:00 AM, or 2:00 PM, or 8:00 in the evening. They happen for four hours at a time, or six, or even eight, if they're expecting a lot of calls. Good thing no one's looking because my wardrobe leaves something to be desired. Entire outfits cost in the neighborhood of $40, and have been carefully culled from New York's finest thrift shops. Whatever rips is sewn, poorly, by me, IQ 139, almost failer of home ec.

Today, I've got on a gray and black abstract print mini with black leggings and purple Doc Marten boots with a top I'm particularly proud of, in a horrible clashing print of red and purple. Why this makes me happy, I don't know. But it sets me apart from the other people on Earth, without a doubt.

I grab two Diet Dr. Peppers out of the fridge (I buy them by the 12 pack, easy-access carton), a banana from the bowl and head out while Felicity is sleeping on the futon in the living room. Her purse is halfway under her head, trying and failing to be a pillow. And her clothes are draped over my desk chair. This can't be fun for her.

I scribble a note, saying that Ron is coming over later. I have no idea where she'll go, but hopefully not home. Over the past 12 or so hours, she's cried three times, raged four, and gone silent even more. It's the silence that scares me most of all.

I leave the note on the floor by the strap of her purse, and wish her no more pain. If this love stuff is beyond her, there's little to no hope for the rest of us.

My shift begins with a call from a woman I can barely hear, though there are clearly whooshing tires and rain behind her. A payphone.

"I'm trying not to get wet," she says, her voice like a little girl's. She's a Leo, born at the end of July.

"What can I answer for you today?"

"I want to ask about a guy."

Don't we all.

"All right, what's this guy's name?"

"Mark."

I shuffle the cards, thinking about a guy named Mark. What does Mark look like and how did he meet this woman? Where is she standing, trying to keep out of the rain?

I try to map out all the possible permutations and births and deaths, comings and goings, and all the energy paths leading up to this moment. And the weird thing is, I can see a lot of it. It just opens up in my mind and I am surprised. It's never happened like that before.

"Do you have a specific question about him, or do you want me to just look at the situation in general?"

"Um . . . I guess general?"

I lay out the cards, the indicator, and then the top and bottom. The past and the future, and the three cards leading up to the conclusion. Fives, sixes, sevens—obstacles, hard work, then a breakthrough.

And right in the middle of it is a queen. I ask if that's her, and get a big NO in my mind, almost as if someone's sitting next to me, speaking it in a normal tone of voice. I have the urge to draw back and tell them to tone it down, but there's no one there. Just the murmur of other psychics talking to similarly lovelorn folks in all corners of the world.

"I can see that he cares about you."

"Really?"

Her voice breaks my heart, and all at once, I know he doesn't. I don't want to lie to her. But for some reason, I want her to be happy, same as everyone.

"Yeah, really." Now I'm sure of it. I can see him cuddling her in my mind's eye, and treating her almost like a doll. "He does like you a lot, and he thinks about you. There is one problem, though. Does he hang around with a woman a lot?"

"Yeah, he has a friend named Dina."

"Have they known each other for a long time?"

"Yeah."

"There's more to their relationship, unfortunately."

"You're kidding. He's cheating on me?"

I can still hear the rain behind her and it sounds so sad coming through the speaker. "I'm not saying that exactly, but she would like to have more of a relationship with Mark, and doesn't seem to have any problem with how that happens."

"God damn it." She's crying now, and I feel like the biggest jerk in the universe.

I say softly, "Do you want me to ask about the future of the relationship, because you're paying almost five dollars a minute." Hopefully, no one's heard that last bit.

She sniffs, blows her nose. "All right."

I shuffle and lay out another spread. "If you want him you can have him, the cards say. But you'll have to fight for him."

As soon as I say it, I know she won't, or she can't. I know they'll stay together for a few more weeks, or a few more months, until they feel strong enough to break apart, and connect with other people.

"I don't know what to do now. But I have to hang up. Thank you."

Then the line goes dead, and I need a break like I've never needed one before.

Ron is waiting on my doorstep when I get home, grinning that sideways grin of his and making me hungry. I'm struggling with two overflowing plastic grocery bags, which he gallantly relieves me of as we climb the stairs. He comments on my cool door (extra points in my book), and I make him some linguine with cilantro pesto. Not exactly homemade pasta, but maybe I'm not there yet in the culinary department.

I realize, when we're sitting on the floor eating the first few bites, that I've forgotten the Parmesan cheese that, as any cook worth his or her salt will tell you, is one of the main fucking ingredients in pesto. He's kind, says it's great, and eats all of his. I can barely choke it down and apologize, maybe a tad on the needy side, about the cheese.

"I didn't even notice it." Then he's kissing me and we're lying on the floor, the garlic smell in the air mingling with the light sweat of his body. "Man, you're beautiful," he breathes. "Look at your hair in this light."

Then we're naked and the sun is going down. If only for the inconvenient detail of the indoor-outdoor carpeting, which is chafing my back something fierce, it would all be perfect and almost magical. "I could do this forever," he says.

The sex is brief but enjoyable, and he's putting on his jeans again. I prop myself up on one elbow, unwilling to let go of the afterglow so quickly.

"Got somewhere to be?" I ask, hoping for a playful tone.

"I have to go meet some people."

"Oh. Sounds important," I tease.

He turns to me, a whole other person. "Look, we're not really to the stage of our relationship where you can say that. So if this is the way it's going to be, then maybe we should think about what we're doing."

Huh?

He's out the door with a peck on the cheek, like I'm his sister or something. I listen to the sound of his motorcycle starting outside in the dusk and know this particular journey has come to an end.

Get your motor runnin', dude.

September
☆ Virgo ☆

I'm getting the hang of it.

For a few days, I'm blindsided by the sudden appearance and disappearance of Ron in my life. I've had mostly boyfriends in my life, not casual hookups, dating partners, bootie calls and the like. I walk through these days in a somber kind of cloud, keeping to myself and watching the phone warily when it rings. I have no desire to pick it up and have an awkward conversation with him.

At work, I've taken to reading books about astrology, as a way to understand people before I get involved, hoping to save a little of the chrome I feel has been stripped away. In between calls, I read about the Moon, always an interesting celestial body:

> *The Moon is considered Void of Course when it's not making any major aspects to other planets. Every few days this happens, as the Moon changes signs. Sometimes, this period can last just a few minutes to a day, or even longer. Relationships, events, jobs and projects begun under a Void of Course Moon are not likely to come to fruition. They may move forward just*

enough to give you the impression of fulfillment, only to
disappoint at the last minute. Waiting until the Moon
has moved into the adjacent sign supports a more positive
outcome.

God, that sounds familiar. I try to remember the date we first talked on the phone, and look it up in the ephemeris. No, not void then. I look up our first date, that evening, and the last time I saw him. Nothing.

Maybe he was scared, or never intended anything serious to come of it. Maybe he's an idiot. Numerous scenarios float through my mind as I sit there, humiliated and looking for answers in an ancient book.

Maybe there is no answer.

Felicity says it's her fault, that she should have looked into his past history, asked more questions. But she was only looking out for me, trying to ease the pain of my breakup and ease me into a new life in a new state. I can't blame her any more than I can blame myself for wanting to meet an interesting new person, which he seemed to be.

The tears dry quickly. After all, I barely knew him. Not really.

I've found, in the weeks I've been at this job, that every day has its own theme. Though people looking for romantic advice usually dominate each day, there are countless sub-sets there. Women, men, cheating and the long-term viability on any given relationship are popular topics.

Today's theme is getting back together with an ex, one of my least favorite.

The call I get right after lunch is a woman with a slight accent named Tess. She sounds European, maybe east of the Urals, and was born under the sign of Virgo.

"I want to ask about Anthony," she says.

I lay out the cards and before I've even gotten the outcome down, I can see that he's no longer in the picture. "Looks like you're not together anymore," I venture.

"No, he left me a few weeks ago."

"I can see that he's very busy in his life."

"Yes, he has a business, but I want to see if he'll come back to me."

I lay down a few more cards: fives, twos, more than a few swords.

"I can't see that happening, I'm sorry to say. He's really focused in another direction now." And I'm getting a mental picture, which I don't want to tell her about, of violence.

"He used to hit me all the time," she sighs. "I thought it was his way of testing me."

Did she just say that?

I say, "He has a problem expressing anger, but it has nothing to do with you."

"Well, what can I do to get him back? I know that it's my fault he left."

I breathe in and out a few times, trying to quiet my shaking hands. The managers have told me I would get calls like this, but this is my first. For some reason, it's deeply unsettling.

"Honestly, Tess, I can't see that you did anything wrong. He just has an issue with being together . . ."

Tactical mistake, I realize, almost as soon as it's out of my mouth.

"Maybe I can help him to be together with me, if I change something. Should I lose more weight? I have been trying to cut down . . ."

I lay down a few more cards, just for show now, and say, "It's his problem, Tess. But I have to be truthful with you. I don't see him coming back. I'm sorry."

"All right, well, goodbye." She sounds disconsolate, empty, spent. Undoubtedly, I've ruined her day.

When I hang up the receiver, I ask for a break, and spend the next few minutes crying in the bathroom. It's not my own life that's bugging me, or even Tess' infinite sadness. It's the incredible futility of love.

Felicity's left me a note when I get home, that she's talked it out with Freddie and is going home to Hollywood. I wonder if my situation with Ron has made her too uncomfortable to stay any longer, but hope I'm wrong about that. As so few of my friends are married, I want them to stay together, to thwart the multiple divorces in my own family's past and do battle with all the romantic pain of the universe.

She's done all the dishes in the sink, no mean feat. In my semi-depressed state, I have not been the most attentive of homemakers. Felicity has also left me some cookies, soda (yay!) and other goodies in the fridge. Nice lady, that. I must remember to keep her around. She's even folded up all the bedding I've lent her, and left it on the couch in a neat pile.

It's cleaner than I recall it being in a long time, thanks to her. I sit on the couch and think about what to do. When you're alone, you have all the time in the world. The hours before and after work start to become large and distorted after such a long time of being with someone. They stretch out endlessly, like a prison sentence.

But I like to think that I am not that easily imprisoned. I live two blocks from the freakin' beach, after all. People pay big money for this stuff, so I shove my feet into a pair of polka-dot flip-flops and head down there.

I've loved Venice Beach even before I moved out here, for its freaks and its poets, its cafés and salty smell. It's easy to imagine the sailors here in the 1940s, fresh from shore leave, and the rippling testosterone cases on Muscle Beach. The light is getting low as I walk along the boardwalk, drawing a coppery sliver along the horizon. A man at the edge of the sidewalk has constructed a life-sized mermaid completely out of sand, with ample breasts and a wasp waist. He's heaping up a little more on her chest, lovingly shaping it into two symmetrical circles, when two kids on skateboards veer a little too close. "Fucking little bastards!" he yells. "You can't see I'm working here?"

Every other stand is a head shop, selling pipes, fringed roach clips and Bob Marley t-shirts. He's like the token saint of pot smokers, apparently, their Jesus and Mary rolled together. There's cheap, ugly jewelry and ponchos and greasy food, and the smells coming off some of them make bile come into my mouth. The homeless guys are grouped along the wall, just next to the food stands, evidently waiting for them to close, or leave the unsold food in a nearby dumpster. One of them holds a neon-green cross, about two feet long, at his side like a sword.

I have nowhere to go, so I walk toward the Ferris wheel I can see in the distance, lit up now that the sun is almost completely down. Part of me has dreamed about this moment, scratching angrily into my high school notebooks. Part of me has planned this all along. But I never thought I would have no one to turn to when the sun went down, no one to grab an ice cream cone with and board the Ferris wheel, giggling.

My shift doesn't begin for another few hours, so I grab some dinner at a local market, a packaged salad I will eat later. When I arrive, I find that I have a new manager, named Delia. She's a tall, rangy redhead with ringlet curls and a crooked smile. I have to admit that I've yet to come across anyone you'd pick out on the street as "psychic." There are no turbans, no flowing robes or crystal balls. All the people I've met so far seem like folks you'd see at a barbecue, heaping potato salad onto a paper plate. They're so regular, in fact, that I have a sneaking suspicion that they're not all that good at what they do, though that could be me projecting. I have not yet completely embraced my "gift" as they call it, and only believe halfway in what I do for a living.

Delia's on a call when I come in, so I put my book bag down quietly, making eye contact and exchanging a little wave with her. I sign onto the network with my code and wait. I toy with opening my salad. I wait. I open a book and close it again. The waiting never ends, and sometimes it makes me antsy.

The sound of Delia's voice is calming and comfortable in comparison. Though I like Radar, being around him makes me nervous. He's so quiet, it's almost like he's not there, and I feel compelled to fill the silence. I know Mercy, of course, but her energy is keyed up and jittery at times, especially when Martin's in the room. This is a nice break.

"All right then, Marlene. My name is Delia, if you need to talk to me again. You take care, now." She hangs up and turns to me, as she writes down her hold time.

"You must be Alyson."

"I am." I get up to shake her hand, and she gives me a warm smile. Then her eyes stray up to the center of my forehead.

"I've heard about your mole," she mentions, smiling.

I'm immediately self-conscious. "My mole?"

"Yeah, you have a little mole right in the middle of your forehead." She points it out with absolutely no malice, as you might to a child with one blue eye and one brown.

"I guess it's always been there."

"You know what it means, though, right?"

"I guess not."

"You have a mark right at your third eye. Don't tell them I told you, but some of the other psychics are scared of you."

"Wow, really? I don't even consider myself psychic. I just read cards."

"Do you see images in your mind when you read?"

"Yes, sometimes. Other times, I just . . . know things."

She smiles again. "You're psychic, all right."

I'm not convinced, but smile at her anyway. She's the nicest manager I've had so far, and I feel comfortable around her, as if I might actually be able to do this and not feel like a fraud.

"You'll see," she says, winking.

I get my first call a few minutes later. Halfway through my salad, I put my fork down and grab my cards, encased in their black velvet pouch. "Hi, how can I help you this evening?"

I'm surprised when it's a man's voice, since most of our callers are women. "I'm worried about my relationship," he confesses. He sounds mature, and I see a gray-haired man in sage-colored clothing, maybe a former athlete with a tennis elbow. He likes to sit by the window in the morning, watching birds. Then the image dissolves.

"I can see that you were with someone you felt very strongly about, but something happened."

I lay down a few more cards. He's not abusive, doesn't drink, isn't cheating on her. "She's not coming back, though. I'm not sure why." There's a Page, right in the middle. "Do you have kids?"

"Her ex-husband murdered our son about a year ago."

All the air rushes out of my lungs, and I feel like I'm going to faint.

"He went to Joe's school, and pretended to be me so he could take him into the woods and kill him. We searched for weeks before the police dogs found his body in a shallow grave."

"Oh my God, I'm so sorry."

"It's strange what you can get used to, if you're given enough time."

I remember why he's called, and that this isn't cheap for him, and lay down a few more cards. "She can't trust you. But I have to say that it's not you. It's not you she can't trust. She can't trust anyone now, and maybe not for a long time."

"I tell her I love her all the time. I want to marry her and take care of her, but she won't let me do any of that now. She just shakes her head and tells me it's not meant to be."

"I wish I had better news for you."

"So there's no chance of us getting back together?"

"I can see that you can be with her, just not in the way you really want. She needs a lot of time to heal. And you would need to decide if you can give her that or not."

"All right then. Thank you for the reading."

"You're welcome. I'll say a prayer for your son."

"Thank you, that's very kind."

He hangs up. I don't know why I said that. I don't know any prayers, can't remember too many of them from my youth, or my stint at a Jesuit college. But the thought was there, the desire to make his pain less intense. Maybe that means something; I don't know.

Delia catches sight of my face. "Got a tough one?'

"Yeah," I breathe. "His son was murdered."

"Oh, gosh. You'll find that you need to protect yourself sometimes, or your energy might get depleted. Some of us get sick from what we put into this work."

I feel full behind the eyes, and am suddenly afraid I'll cry in front of my new manager. I just never expected that kind of call when I signed up for this job. The other psychic on this shift has her back to us, twirling her hair in her index finger and ignoring our conversation. I wish I could be like her, I think, armored, immune and untouched. But it's no more in my nature than it is to erase that image of a little boy, alone in the woods, from my mind.

From there, my readings get easier. I have a middle-aged woman looking to turn her life around and start dating after the death of her husband, a young woman who wants to get out of her house and go to college, and a twenty-something guy looking to find his soulmate. It's all so human and normal that I'm touched when I feel like I'm helping someone, or doing any good at all.

Delia gives me a break, and I walk down the hall, catching sight of a few people organized into cubicles, like us. At this time of night. Weird.

Outside, I stare up at the sky, bright with a low-hanging garland of stars. For a few seconds, I wish I smoked, so I could have those few romantic moments of contemplating the universe.

But my reality isn't romantic. It's as real as it gets, and I'm not sure I'm ready to be that mature. Too late to get anyone else to handle it for me, and I have to pay my rent. So I go back inside, *sans* cigarette, ready for the next wave of folks needing some perspective, on something or other. I'm ready, for some reason, thinking it *is* pretty amazing what you can get used to, given the time.

Virgo, the organizer, known for its anal-retentive ways and ability to compartmentalize its behaviors, friends and beliefs into well-ordered cubicles. They are the health nuts, the fasters and yoga aficionados of the zodiac.

I meet one of them not long after Ron has made for the hills, at the gym. Before I left New York, I made sure that I could transfer my gym membership to a partner site in Los Angeles. On the first day I actually make it there, a dark-haired muscle rippled guy named Irman checks me in.

"We don't take these cards anymore," he says, dismissing me.

"Yeah, you do." I hate it when people do that.

"Who says?"

"My gym in New York, that's who." I stand there, leveling my gaze at him until he smiles.

"You're from New York?"

"That's right." I refuse to break eye contact.

His eyes linger on mine. "Let's see what we can do, then."

He taps something into a computer, scans the page, enters a code. He takes my card, enters the information, and hands it back to me. "There you go, Alyson. You're in the system."

"Thanks ever so much," I say, grabbing the card and sweeping into the women's locker room without a look back.

I change quickly, notice that there's a kind of satellite workout room in the back of the locker room, where a few sad-looking women are pedaling and chugging at the machinery. There's a woman with enormous melon tits staring at herself in the mirror (completely bare breasted) while she blow-dries her hair.

I make for the floor, choosing a stationary bike and pedaling up a sweat within a few minutes. Listening to people's problems all day has made me blocked up, stuffed with images of murdered children and standing in the rain, asking about men who don't love them back. I am staring straight ahead, used to the etiquette of the weight room, not willing to give anyone an excuse to come over and talk to me.

Then there's a body beside me. Someone large, larger than I am, with long dark hair.

"We got off on the wrong foot," he says. I turn to find Irman standing beside me, not bothering to hide the fact that he's looking right at my cleavage, which has got to be pretty sweaty by now.

"We're on some kind of foot?" I can't help it. He's pissed me off, and now I can't keep my mouth shut. That, combined with Ron's sudden assholeyness, has me irritated.

He leans a little closer, and I can feel his breath on my earlobe. "I'd hoped so."

I make eye contact again, bat my eyelashes for effect, and laugh.

"Come up with something better than that and try again."

He sulks off to his station, wounded, but I don't care.

The next afternoon, I'm back at work, working with a girl named Opal, who I know a little bit through Mercy. In her spare time, she works at the same aromatherapy store, giving readings and doing healings. She's a Sagittarius, like me, and it's hard for us to sit near each other when we're working, because we get too silly and excited. I try to finish my book, so I can return it to the library, but she keeps drawing pictures of me, with little hearts and flowers all around, or passes me notes written in childish scrawl.

"You have to come with me this weekend. I'm going to see if we can read at this new tea house in West Hollywood."

"All right, maybe."

"No, not maybe. Yes, Ally my pally."

My phone rings. "Hi, this is Bronwyn. How can I help you?"

"I'm worried about my son."

"OK, then. Let me get your first name."

"Dottie."

"And your date of birth."

"9/11/52."

"All right, Dottie. Let me take a look . . . ," I shuffle quickly, feeling her energy, tight and twisted, through the phone line.

The cards go down in a row, and just as I'm about to lay down the last one, The Moon pops out of the deck, and flops down last. I stare at it for a few seconds, and lay down the card at the top of the deck—Five of Wands.

"I can see that you've been having some disagreements lately."

"Not really."

I look again. Five, sixes—trouble at home.

"Your son has a lot of friends."

"Yes, he's with new people all the time. He's very popular."

"But there are a few of them . . ." I pause, searching for the most diplomatic words I can muster. "A few of them, I'm not sure you want him to be around."

"Why?"

I lay down two more cards. That's why The Moon came out to play. Five of Cups and The Devil.

"Are you sure your son isn't involved with drugs or alcohol?"

"He's only thirteen!" I hold the phone away from my ear, she's so loud.

"I'm sorry, Dottie, but that's what I see. I would suggest keeping an eye on him."

"You don't know what you're talking about. He's too young for all that."

"Can I answer anything else for you?"

"I don't think so. Good day," she says, tight-lipped and angry. The phone bangs down in my ear, though now, I've come to expect it, at least some of the time.

I turn away from my phone with a confused look on my face. Delia's flipping through a magazine, and raises her eyes to meet mine. I look back at the cards on my desk.

"You all right?"

"I think so. But I'm trying to figure out how I could be so wrong about what I saw."

"What makes you think you're wrong?"

"She said it."

"Then she hung up on you?"

"Yeah." For a second, I feel like I'm going to cry. I just can't seem to get the hang of this, and don't believe on any level I'm a "real" psychic. I'm being paid barely above minimum wage, and nothing is as I thought it would be.

Delia gets up, comes around the side of her desk, and squats by the edge of mine.

Quietly, she says, "When we get closer to the truth, they can feel it, and most of the time, they don't like it. You may not be right all of the time, but you wouldn't be here if it weren't for the fact that you're good at what you do. You understand?"

I shake my head slowly, fighting like hell not to let the tears fall out of my eyes. I can see Opal staring at me from across the room, too scared to say anything silly in front of Delia.

"You have a gift, and you'll find that it gets stronger here. All of us have found out how much more we can do. We learn more just by coming to work. You'll see."

"OK," I manage.

"For the record, her son's already done drugs, probably about three times. Mostly pot." She winks at me, goes back to her seat, and flips through the magazine as if nothing's happened.

I wish I could have one of those winning moments, when I toss my hair back and face the world with a cheeky grin. I wish I could be Mary Tyler Freakin' Moore. But I'm still a little shaky. I turn back to my book, breathe in and out very slowly until I can feel my heart beginning to stop clunking around.

I want to quit so badly I can taste it. But amidst all the mental chatter, the back and forth of common sense and incipient recklessness, one part of me remembers that look on Delia's face, of complete calm and acceptance of what she has, that thing that links all of us in this room. No one's faking it when we come here. There may be confusion and suffering and turmoil in our lives, in the world. But we are real. And I have to find a way to be all right with joining their ranks.

I'm tired when I get home, and crack open a beer and sit on my impossibly small futon couch. I'm too tired to think about sharing it with anyone right now. The beer is drained, and then another, and I realize I need to clean my place. I have a friend coming to visit from New York, and she'll be here tomorrow evening.

I slip some Staple Singers into the tape player and let Mavis' voice fill the room. Yellow rubber gloves stretch to my elbows as I plunge my hands into the steaming water and scrub the sinkful of dishes that has been sitting there for a few days. I'm not a complete slob by nature, but living alone has tested the tensile strength of my cleanliness. Soon, the dishes are sitting in my new drying rack, looking fresh and gleaming.

I move to my desk, heaped with paper, letters, books and printouts from the library. I'm thinking about writing a new screenplay based on mythology, but the plot isn't coming yet, so all I have is a heap of stuff to work from and no filing cabinet. Piling it on the floor feels too college dorm room, so I line the books up at the edge of the desk—there, that's better—and pile the papers and letters on top of the notebooks. I buy them in stacks of five because my dreams have become so much more vivid since my new job began.

The tape ends, and I throw in a mix tape made by a friend in New York. On a confused, drunken night on my rooftop, we'd hooked up, a little I guess, and now I have no idea where we stand. His letters don't let on that he's worried about it, and his tapes have gotten me, relatively sane, across a country filled with crap radio.

Blondie leads into Hank Williams, which segues into The Ventures.

I'm torn between drinking another beer and dusting this room. I can finish the rest tomorrow, right? And the bathroom has to be last because, well, cleaning bathrooms sucks. I eye the refrigerator. I wish I had a cigarette, drinking being the only time I smoke at all. No, I don't want my apartment to smell like smoke. Nothing less sexy on earth.

I grab the dust rag and cleanser, and get to work on the one item that needs dusting—the "entertainment" center, an Ikea product of black painted wood about two shelves high. It takes about twenty seconds to do, then I jump up and down to Public Image, trying to swat the cobwebs out of the corners.

At the end of my cleaning, I'm filled with energy. Figures.

I don't have a kitchen table, so I sit on the floor, the *LA Weekly* spread out before me. It seems like there are about half the number of movies here, because they're stacked up in multiplexes, with very few independent options. Clubs are another matter, though I have to get used to the 2:00 AM last call, when it's always been 4:00 AM in New York.

Lots of bands I want to see, but none tonight. I close the paper and think about doing an aerobics tape, to get my ya-yas out before bed. In this state, there's no way I'm going to fall asleep. I think about calling Felicity, to see how she's doing with Freddie, but get scared that the news may not be good. I take out my address book and scan the list of New York friends. Who's still likely to be up at this hour? Most of them, probably.

Picking up the phone, I wave goodbye to my weekly budget. Those are made to be broken anyway.

With the cleaning complete, even the bathroom, I put away the last of my laundry and grab my keys. I have to pick up Tina at LAX, and I have a very sketchy idea of how to get there, or where to park. According to my new *Thomas Guide*, which cost half of my weekly food budget, I can drive through Marina del Rey, catch Lincoln through Playa Vista, past Loyola Marymount until I dovetail with Sepulveda, which will take me to the airport. It's bound to be faster than the freeway, which so far has proven to be more of a parking lot than a venue for successful travel. Feeling like I know my way to the airport makes me feel groovy and with it, almost a native.

As I round the corner of my building on the way to the parking lot, I see it. Someone has spray-painted an indecipherable tag on the thin, grayish column of a palm tree. The red is too garish to be mistaken for the ketchup blood of horror movies, too vibrant to be anything other than man-made. As I strap myself into the baking seat of my aging V.W., I wonder why someone would covet a palm tree so fiercely that he would mark it as his own.

I recognize Tina right away when she gets off the plane. Though she's gained some weight in the past few months, she grabs me in a big hug. "Look at you," she says. "You look fantastic!"

"Oh, thanks."

"You're so tan!'

"Really? It's completely unintentional. I walk sometimes on the beach."

"Have you seen him?"

I know who she means immediately. "No, that's done."

She looks at her shoes for a minute.

"Anyway, do you need to get your bag?"

We move down the escalator to baggage claim, and the tangle of limo drivers carrying cards with last names. I can see her scanning them for any famous people, then fall into step behind her as she veers toward the carousel.

"I wasn't sure what you wanted to do, so I kind of collected a few things."

"Well, I'm going to try to get in touch with Tony's publicist so I can do the interview." She stops short of saying that this is why she's come, though it's pretty clear from her face.

"I need to go to the gym later, if you want to chime in on that."

"Sure, yeah. I could use a workout."

Her bag comes careening off the belt, with the help of an enormous black man who looks slightly like Mister T in his bouncer days. He gives her an appreciative grin as she snaps the handle into place and wheels it away. His eyes stay locked to her ass as we walk away.

But she's oblivious. She wants this rock star she's come to vanquish, and the interview is the way in. I am obviously an appendage, a place to stay, an unwilling wing-woman. Fabulous.

We drop off her stuff and get changed before heading off to the gym. I'm used to this—shoehorning workouts in between weird shifts, going first thing in the morning, in the middle of the night—whenever I can get my heart pumping and my energy moving is good enough. She, on the other hand, is more . . . um, high maintenance, requiring some time to relax, a glass of water, and a fresh pair of underwear before she's ready to go and sweat.

Irman's at the front desk when we walk in, and he doesn't waste any time.

"I want to bring a guest today," I say, trying to cut through any bullshit right off the bat.

He eyes me up and down, obviously, without shame. "Your membership doesn't let you have guests."

"What are you talking about? I asked about this before I left New York, and they said I could bring as many guests as I wanted, as long as they signed in and left an address and phone number . . . probably so you can harass them later, right?"

This is apparently a turn on for him. His face breaks into a slow grin, and he slides a guest pass across the desk. Tina looks at him, then to me, then back to him.

"Thanks," I say, pocketing the pass and indicating for her to sign in on the clipboard. "You can leave a fake address and number, if you want," I say, loud enough for him to hear.

She gives him the clipboard and he scans down to her name. "Debbie Harry, cute."

I give him a big smile.

"That attitude's going to get you in trouble one day," he calls after me, as I make my way to the locker room.

"Hasn't so far," I reply.

I stash my stuff in a locker and am about to head out the door when Tina hangs back. She eyes the satellite workout area in the back of the women's locker room. "I think I'm going to stay here," she says.

"Really? All the main equipment is out there."

"Yeah, it's just, calmer in here."

"All right. I'll see you in around an hour then. Meet me back here?"

"Sure." I watch as she straddles an exercise bike and begins pedaling, very slowly, to I don't know where.

I have a lot to work off, with my head in my writing and this guest in my home. I've been living alone for a few months now, establishing rhythms and getting used to my own company. Not that I'm not glad to see her, but it seems like she's not really here to see me. Not really.

I mount the Stairmaster and stab in my weight, the desired time and fitness level. I move my legs up and down in time with the top-40 music bleating from the crummy speakers overhead. I should have brought my own Walkman, because the best I can hope for is "Hot Blooded" from this station.

My mind wanders. I open the book I've brought, but *The Gnostic Gospels* is too ambitious for today. My mind jumps around. There is the heaviness of my eyelids, the memory and worry of my insomnia. There's my job, the worry over money, then a distraction—a hazel-eyed, boyish-looking guy using the bicep machine across the room. His forehead wrinkles with the effort required to hoist the chrome plates and bang them decisively down after each rep. There's something about his jawline that reminds me of a lover, left long ago, and our last tryst in a cab. Late night, New York, rain streaking the windows. His lips closing around my bare nipple, his fingers sliding over my belly and then under my panties, contacting my everything.

I shiver. There are bright, proud bodies all around me, pumping, pushing, contorting. The place is awash in pheromones. It reeks of raunch and genitals and sex. *Ten minutes to go.*

Tinny disco music hisses into the room. Harsh light ricochets over the serious, shining surfaces, exponentially reflecting the sparkling on hard brows, pecs, abs all around me. Blood sings in my veins, and my heart pumps like a derrick working the earth.

I do thirty minutes on the treadmill, alternating walking and running. A year ago, I couldn't even do that, with my asthma exacerbated by the smallest growth on the admittedly rare trees. Now I can do that and thirty minutes of weight training. You couldn't really call me muscle bound, but I do all right.

Everywhere I look, there I am. Mirrors send my reflection back endlessly, diminishing my form until it's gone. I pump metal plates up and down with my legs, feeling the muscles inflate with blood. Life rushes faster through my veins.

I make eye contact with no one. I am focused on this work, on the functioning of my body. I feel strong, in control. Alive.

I finish my last set, wipe off the machine with a towel, and look up. Irman is standing on the balcony above, staring down at me. His face doesn't say anything but *I see you*, and *I know you*, and *I'm going to win one day, you just wait.*

I stare back for a few seconds, mostly to let him know that I've seen him staring. He doesn't shift his gaze. Bastard.

In the locker room, I take a quick shower and change into a sundress. It's not just the heat that makes me wear less here. It's the climate, the acceptance range of behavior. The culture of nakedness that's somehow expected. I'm not exactly naked, though.

"Isn't that kind of short?" Tina asks, a comical kind of horror on her face.

"That's why I've got the tights," I say, pulling on short leggings underneath. Boots go on after. I can't give them up so easily.

I can tell she doesn't approve, but I don't care. She's wearing tight warm-ups with a t-shirt pulled down so far it actually accentuates her ass.

Outside, she's already complaining. She needs some clean underwear. She needs some frozen yogurt and water. I have to make a call, to see if Opal needs me to cover her shift tomorrow. She's not home and I leave a silly message. Before I can hang up, Irman's by my side, brushing my hand with his fingertips.

"You look nice," he says. Lazily, he scratches his ultra-cut deltoid with a thumb. His eyes alternate, first fastening on my breasts, then sneaking over to catch a glimpse of himself in the mirror, then connecting, laserlike, with my ass.

"Thanks."

Tina does the ping-pong glancing, back and forth, back and forth.

He tries to slip something into my hand—a business card.

"What's this?"

"My number."

I look at it, smile, and hand it back to him.

As we walk away, he calls after me, "I'll just have to call you, then."

When we get back home, I can see that the tree tagging has escalated. Since that morning, someone has smeared white paint over the red markings, leaving a primitive, stippled canvas on the trunk. Over that is a symbol like two oval-shaped eyes, with parallel lines extending out like gunfire from them. I point it out to Tina, who grunts to express its lack of impression on her. She lives in Brooklyn, where anything is fair game, and everything can be festooned in loud, menacing colors.

"I have to get inside and call his publicist," she says, with an urgency I don't understand.

We go inside and she places her call.

I'm lying on my bed, paging through a novel when she hangs up. She stands in the doorway, looking a lot happier than a few minutes ago.

"How'd it go?"

"It might happen on Sunday, but she's not sure yet."

"Well, that's better than no, right?

She nods, perches on the edge of the bed. "Can you read my cards?"

I have done this a million times for her, but she has also done some of the same for me, in the days following my breakup. I hoist myself up and locate my bag, which has tried to wedge itself into the crack between the crappy plastic table acting as a nightstand and the wall. I liberate the cards, and she's already shuffling.

"How could he have married someone like her? I mean, he's nothing like her."

The rapper she's interested in has recently wed an actress of limited talent and unquestionable beauty. Tina's supposed to interview him in five days, after much haranguing and manipulation, for a well-known music publication that sported no credentials but a young staff willing to slave for bottom dollar, and relied on the support of the publisher's enormous trust fund to continue its daily operations.

I lay out the cards on the rumpled covers, trying not to wince at what I see. "He's really busy," I manage. "Looks like he's about to be traveling as well."

"He'd better wait until he meets me!" I can see that she's not kidding.

I wonder what she thinks is going to happen. Locked stares over coffee, lips intertwining over her tape recorder?

"You definitely have chemistry." She brightens at that.

"Margaret said their marriage probably wasn't even real. It's probably just a publicity stunt. She even said his wife might be a lesbian."

It should be said that Tina is living with someone I know, the drummer in my ex-boyfriend's band. It should be said, but it won't, because she's my friend, and I have no idea what she's planning.

"What will you do . . . I mean, what if you're attracted to each other when you meet? What are you going to do?"

"I'd sleep with him," she says evenly.

"Even though you live with someone?"

Curtly, Tina nods. Her jaw is set, under a line of fat that extends beneath her chin. She is adamant and challenging.

"Looks like it's a successful interview. But there could be a delay."

"I don't want to hear that!"

"It's right there. The patience card. Just go slow, and let it happen."

She snatches the cards up and starts shuffling again. I turn to look out the window. The sun is going down and my stomach is already rumbling. The view looks magnificent from here and I can smell the salt coming off the ocean. How cool is that?

"Can you just see what he's going to think of me when we meet?" I spread the cards again, and it seems like I'll never stop doing this—at work, for friends, for myself. The cards will keep accumulating until they reach the horizon line, reach around the globe, extending into the sky.

Either way, she'll have confirmation or rejection of her crush within a few days. Either way, she'll know. Until then, no amount of conversation, no cocoon of words, will shelter her from her insecurity.

I go out early the next morning for muffins and coffee. Since I don't drink it, I don't have a coffee machine, which tends to irk the shit out of anyone who stays with me. I understand. My caffeinated beverage is soda, and I drink them unapologetically throughout the day.

The painted symbol on the palm tree has been dominated by two towering red initials, leaning together like a couple of drunks in the road. I want to take a picture of it or something, somehow document this tiny feud erupting between two people over a tree.

When I walk in, Tina's on the phone. Her face shades from hopeful to ashen within the space of seconds. She's in tears when she replaces the receiver. Tony's unable to see her, the publicist says, due to his busy schedule. There will be a new record in the fall, and she will be among their first calls for interviews at that time. Until then, he has nothing to say. Tina is crushed.

We spend the rest of the morning, and most of the afternoon, reading tarot cards and trying to figure out why she's traveled three thousands miles on the most insubstantial of ruses. But my efforts are futile. Nothing short of a miracle will make her feel any better.

At five thirty the next morning, I take her to the airport. The red initials on the tree have been whited out, made insignificant by the two eyes design, which spills off the edges of the back and into the side of the building. It feels like a warning. Don't fuck with the eyes.

In the terminal we hug, but Tina feels like wet laundry. She hasn't showered, and her hair has the thick, chemical smell of smog. It's unlike her.

As I watch her walking away, into the depths of the light, and the people, and the rushing of LAX, I wonder how any of us fall in love. Do we have to be in the same room, or can we love someone we've never met? Do they have the same power to hurt us, or are we excused from connecting with phantoms so our hearts will be ready for the real thing?

Maybe I'll never know. I drown my sorrows in Diet Coke, thinking about Tina's sad ride home to Brooklyn. I need the caffeine for my shift, which starts not too long from now.

October
☆ Libra ☆

I am tested.

I know it's going to be a long day when I get my first call. I can just feel it, coming through the telephone wires like bad news.

He sounds pleasant enough, with a voice smooth as a tenor's and a polite, Southern way about him. He even hands over his name and date of birth without a lot of attitude.

"Wonderful, John. Can I answer a particular question for you today?"

"Yes, I'm wondering about a relationship I'm in."

"All right, then. Let me just shuffle the cards, and you tell me when to stop."

I shuffle the cards. "Stop," he says, managing to sound polite when he does so.

I lay them out, up, down, across and up again, letting the images unfold in my mind. I'm getting used to the rhythm of the callers, and am starting to anticipate what they want before they ask for it.

Something troubles me, though, and my eyes zoom right to the center. The Empress. Maybe she's nurturing? Pregnant? Maternal?

"Well, I can see that this is a very rich relationship, and has a lot of closeness in it."

"Yes, we get along great."

"I can see that she's been a little distant recently, but that shouldn't last much longer. She's going through some personal troubles. Nothing that relates to you."

"I hope she's all right."

I throw down a few more cards and it jumps out at me again, as if the card were literally levitating off the desk. Trouble in paradise.

"There's an issue between you, some reason you can't be together."

"Umm hmm . . ." All right, he's not talking.

"I can see that if she could, she'd want to be with you. But she just can't."

"Why not?" He sounds so sad, I have an urge to hug him.

"I wish I could see that for you, but I'm not getting it. Sorry. I can't see that it has anything to do with you, if that makes you feel any better."

"She's my mom," he says, and the world seems to stop.

Did he just fucking say that?

"She's your mom," I repeat, not trusting myself to say anything more. "That definitely explains why she feels she can't be with you."

I'm completely repulsed, and have to shove down the urge to vomit. I wanted to hug this guy a few minutes ago. Christ.

"Can you see if we have a future together?"

Should I tell this guy to take a hike, and see a therapist? Should I cut off the little money I'm making so he'll call right back and talk to someone else?

I'm not prepared for this moment, so I shuffle the cards in one hand and lay out another small reading to the side.

My voice is stuck in my throat, and I have to clear it lightly before I can go on. "I can see that you have a lot of struggles ahead. A lot of obstacles. So no, I don't see you being together in this lifetime." I have to resist the urge to add "sorry" at the end.

"The thing is, she's pregnant." *Ding*—the Empress.

I'm gonna fall off my chair. Faint, go projectile, something.

"She wants to have the baby, but I don't. Do you think she's going to have it anyway?"

A few more cards go down and Jesus H., she's gonna do it. "Yes, it looks like it."

I don't even sound like myself. My voice is far away, stripped of its strength.

"All right, then. Thanks for your help." He rings off with his manners intact.

I could walk right past this guy in the grocery store, I think. He'd be the one buying diapers and formula for the kid with his mom.

No amount of reading can get this guy out of my mind, so I have to try something different. Martin is off today, which means that things are little more relaxed than usual. Katie's the only other reader on duty, and Mercy's usually game. When we don't have any calls, I try to tune in a decent radio station. You'd think it wouldn't be hard in the nation's second largest media market, but just like everywhere else, the airwaves are jammed with the same shit, no matter which direction you turn the knob. Finally, I land on a station playing my favorite Nirvana song that, as far as I know, hasn't been on any of their records:

And if you fool yourself
You will make him happy
He'll keep you in a jar
Then you'll think you're happy
He'll give you breathing holes
Then you will seem happy

I've got too much energy, so I'm up on the nearest chair, a battered black office model with wheels on the bottom. Katie's laughing at me as I gyrate on it, trying not to fall off or careen into a wall. Mercy's torn between being the manager, you can see it on her face, and being my friend. She thinks it's hilarious, though. Her wide face opens in giggles.

My eyes are closed, imagining being in this jar with breathing holes, or a laundry room, or whatever the hell this song is about. I don't care. All that matters is that I am moving out of this room, in my mind at least, into the world of music. It has meant everything to me for most of my life, and if I had any damn talent at all, I probably would have started a band a long time ago. For now, this is it. My head, my heart knocking against my ribs, my ears full of this sound.

The song ends, and when I try to jump off the chair, it skitters out from under me. My ankle twists as I hit the floor.

"Shit," Mercy says, diving for the radio. She twists the volume down as I limp to my seat. Katie's still laughing, her back jiggling up and down in silence. I hear the footsteps Mercy's reacting to, and bury my nose in a book.

It's Patrice, early for her shift, and we all heave a sigh of relief. I've heard that she's originally from Israel, but haven't met her yet.

71

She sniffs the air when she walks in. "Has someone been smoking in here?"

Mercy is the only one who occasionally sneaks a cigarette when she's alone, so we all know this is directed at her.

Katie breaks the silence. "No one's smoking, Sensitive. Get your butt in here."

Patrice walks in, her long nose pointed down in my direction. "Hey, I'm Alyson," I say, sticking out my hand.

She looks at it like it's diseased, but shakes it like you would in Edwardian times, twisting my hand upright and taking just the fingertips in hers.

"I thought we were starting Martin's astrology class today."

"No, he's off. I think it's going to start next week."

Patrice makes a face. She pulls up the chair I've recently been dancing on, and I can see that Katie's trying not to laugh. It takes a wise ass to know one, and she's one in spades.

"I will have to wait until my shift starts, then," Patrice says, as if the midnight train to Cannes has been cancelled, leaving her stranded in Monaco. It's a tough world.

Luckily, I don't get any more calls, and am free to go soon after.

As I pack up my things, Mercy says, "I don't know if you know about Martin's class. He's going to teach us all about astrology, right after this shift every Monday, if you're interested."

A free class in astrology, which I've been meaning to learn anyway? I'm absolutely interested. I tell her that I'll be there next week, and leave them to gossip, and even dance, if they want. Just leave me my chair, if you're kind.

I'm off on Tuesday, so I throw on my workout clothes and head to the gym first thing. Irman's standing at the front desk when I walk in, his black hair hanging lankly over one eye as he copies information from a membership card into the guest book.

I sign in, hoping to slip away, and his hand snakes across the counter to grab my wrist. I jump as he closes his hand around my tattoo. He moves his thumb over the ink, applying pressure to see if it rubs off, I guess.

I try to pull back, but his fingers clamp down harder.

"Is that a tattoo?" he asks. Rather stupidly, it seems to me.

He releases my hand. "Where'd you get it?"

"London."

At least he lets me work out in peace, and only when I emerge from the locker room after a quick shower does he surprise me, by pushing his face into my wet hair.

"You smell . . ."

"What are you doing?"

". . . wonderful." His short, callused fingers catch the hem of my dress and yank gently. "You're a smart ass, aren't you?"

"Some people just call me stupid."

He laughs. "Okay, smart ass. But I still like your tattoo."

I send him a smile of challenge. "Hold that thought."

He raises a play fist. "Maybe you need another tattoo. Where do you want it?"

I point to my butt and run to the elevator.

He bolts after me, winding past stunned customers, all the way to the elevator. I make it inside, push the down button frantically, until the doors kiss shut just as he reaches them.

I have no idea why I do these things. At the time, it seems funny.

I'm driving home when an image of New York hits me, square in the chest. Some of my favorite things there just don't translate to a life in Los Angeles. A small party on a rooftop in the depths of summer, conversations overheard while walking anywhere (it's just not done here), the perfect bagel smothered in scallion cream cheese, the way the air smells like burning wires during a thundershower. It's as if someone has just told me that a lover is dead, or a friend. I know I've lost something, deeply, and have to choke back tears to keep my vision from going blurry.

Pulling over to the curb, I run into a liquor store and buy a handful of cheesy postcards—people on the beach with their asses hanging out of thongs, aging guys on surfboards, a few nature scenes, images of famous intersections. I can't find a pen in my bag so I buy one of those as well, the kind where the woman strips when you turn the pen upside down.

In the car, I let the tears come down as I scribble notes to all my friends who would understand. I write to half a dozen people before I tuck the postcards and pen into the little paper bag and start back home. At least for a few more minutes, I feel connected to people who know me on some level, and can trace my evolution back to the place I began.

At work, I finish the rest of the cards. It's my first shift with Wilma, a striking woman with flaming red hair and blue eyes like a pair of satellite dishes on her face. She is quieter than most managers, preferring not to talk much between calls. I'm fine with that, because I need to finish these cards, and a little bit of writing I want to get done so I can feel like I'm doing something more than helping with the world's romantic issues.

But after a few slow hours, I'm finished with the postcards, the writing, and even reading a novel I've brought along for the ride. Wilma's sitting at her desk, gazing down at its surface, like a switched-off robot.

"So, where are you from?"

She looks up slowly, and my heart freezes when she makes eye contact. There's nothing behind her eyes. Just blank space and emptiness. For a few seconds, I'm actually scared of her. "Originally, I'm from Ohio. But I'm a walk-in."

Maybe I should know what that means. But I don't. "What's that?"

"I was out in the desert a few years ago in the middle of the night, and an alien walked into my body."

Huh. "What did that feel like?" I ask.

"At first, I was confused, but then the alien took over, and it's been in control of me ever since."

"Like little green men aliens?" I'm trying for playful, but her stony look tells me I have a lot to learn.

"No, these aliens aren't green. They're cosmic intelligence, Alyson, and they live in my body."

"So everything you were before . . ."

"It's gone. They gave me a new name, and I'm that person now."

I'm curious, and have a host of questions. But I also don't want her to get mad at me. Not when she has my meager employment in her grasp.

"Wow, that sounds really interesting." I know it's lame, but I have no idea what to say next. I really don't. And it's not like she's trying to get me to join up or anything, take one for the team.

Wordlessly, she goes to the small television and snaps it on. I can't tell if she's angry or just anti-social, so I return to my book. Over my shoulder, I can hear a *Star Trek* rerun, which she sits back to watch at deafening volume.

My phone rings a few seconds later, and I am grateful for the reprieve.

"This is Bronwyn, how can I help you tonight?"

"I need to get a reading about my love life."

"All right, I just need to get your first name and date of birth, please."

"Richard, 10/4/72."

"Do you want to ask about a particular person, or just in general?"

"No, I want to ask about someone named Renetta."

"All right, let's see what comes up for Renetta." I think about her as I shuffle the cards and lay out the Celtic Cross. It hits me again, right at the center of the reading. The Empress. The relationship itself isn't bad, just the creepy feeling I start to get from that card, normally a positive sign of growth and renewal at the center of the spread. But it doesn't sound like the same guy at all. His voice is completely different.

"I can see that Renetta is someone you're very close to, and even though there seems to be a bit of an age difference, that's not an issue with you guys going forward."

"That's good to hear."

"There is one problem, which seems to be another person in the picture. Are you dating someone else as well?"

"Well, I've been thinking about it."

I lay down a few more cards, and all of a sudden, the swords come out. Not a good sign for a relationship. "There's a kind of competition here, or something like that. Almost as if these two people know each other."

"Oh, they do. One is my aunt—we've been dating for awhile—but then I've been thinking about trying to have a three-way with my mother."

This time, I'm not going to just sit there. "Are you kidding?" I ask.

"She's hot," he answers. "You should see her."

I am silent for a few seconds, trying to decide what to say, if anything, or whether to end the call and walk out the door forever. I could probably do this somewhere else, right?

"So, do you think I should go ahead and have the three-way with her?"

"No, I don't." I don't even try to hide my disgust.

"Why not?" he demands.

"Because it's screwed up and wrong. Do you have any other questions tonight?"

"Well, if you're going to be that way about it, no." The phone clatters in my ear.

This is starting to not seem weird to me, most troubling of all.

Thankfully, the phone rings again just a few seconds later. I'm hoping against hope it's not him again. It's not.

"Yeah, is this the psychic?"

"Yes, my name is Bronwyn."

"Bratwurst?"

"No, Bronwyn. How can I help you?"

"I need to find out if Rae-kwon cheating on me."

"All right, I just need your first name and date of birth."

"Quanisha, August 11, 1978."

The cards go down—flip, flip, flip. "Is this guy your boyfriend?'

"Aren't you supposed to tell me dat?"

"OK, then. I can see that you guys may have gone out once or twice, but it doesn't look like you have an exclusive arrangement."

"Arrangement? What that mean?"

"It doesn't look like you've agreed to be together exclusively."

"I don't know what he's doing. That's what I want to know. That's why I'm calling."

"I can see that he does see other women from time to time."

"So he's cheating on me?"

"Well, no. Like I said, it doesn't look like you're exclusive, at least not to him. Take that how you will."

The TV is still blaring, and I try to cover the mouthpiece with my hand when I'm not talking. Wilma is in a trance, staring at the screen like it's a holy oracle. I try to get her attention to turn it down, but she doesn't see me.

"So . . . do he love me?"

I shuffle again, lay out a few more cards. "No, he don't, doesn't. Sorry . . ."

Jesus. I just said that. I half expect her to run to the NAACP and have me arrested. But it doesn't seem to faze her a bit.

"Do Christopher love me?"

A few more cards get added to the pile.

"He's seeing someone now, and I think they have a kid."

"Yeah, Shay just had a baby a few months back. How about Ronald? Do he love me?"

I only have a few more cards in the deck, and they get thrown down on top of the rest. "He's interested in you sexually, but I can't see that developing into anything right away . . ."

"So he don't love me now?"

"No, I'm sorry to say. Did you want me to ask about anything else tonight?

"What's that sound in the background? You watchin' TV or something?"

"No, maybe it's interference on the line." I wave my hand frantically at Wilma now, and make a lowering gesture. She rises, reluctantly, and lowers the volume by a tiny fraction.

"I want to ask about Kevin. Do he love me?"

I take the entire deck back into my hands and shuffle them, then lay out five in a row. Man, she's the unluckiest person in love ever, maybe.

"He's pretty preoccupied with himself now. Looks like he's looking for work, maybe starting a new project, and he may not even be around in your area much longer."

"Yeah, he told me he was going to move to New York."

"Maybe it's best to spend some time on yourself now."

"All right, then. Thank you Bronella."

Maybe that should be my psychic name. Easier to pronounce. More memorable. It's got potential.

When I get off the call and total my hold time, Wilma is standing at the doorway, looking through the office across from us, out to the night sky. The way she's staring, it's like a woman waiting for her husband to return from a dangerous seafaring voyage, or a child yearning for his father to come back from a protracted war. There's a kind of longing that's not passive at all.

"What are you looking at?"

"I have to find the Mother Ship," she answers. Her eyes sweep the horizon, back and forth, back and forth, searching for signs of intelligent life in an upside-down world.

All I want is a beer and a bed when I get home around midnight. The light on my answering machine is blinking, but I don't even care who's called. I'm gazing into the refrigerator for inspiration when the phone rings. I walk over to it, beer in hand.

"Hello?"

Irman's voice slithers out like motor oil. "Where have you been? I've called like seven times."

"Hello to you, too. I've been at work, unlike some people."

"You gotta meet me at lunch tomorrow. I got these temporary tattoos."

"Good for you," I say, yawning.

"No, seriously, you have to meet me."

"Are you asking me out on a date?"

"I'm sorry, I think I got carried away. It's just that . . . well, you're . . ."

"I'm what?'

"I want to tattoo you. I want to kiss your neck for twenty minutes and not let you touch me, even if you beg."

"Fascinating. Look, I'm really tired, and I think I have enough tattoos for one woman. I'm going to sleep . . ."

His voice drops an octave, Barry White sultry. "All alone?"

How he talks me into it, I'll never remember.

I don't fuss with my attire the next day—it's coming off anyway. Black shorts, fishnets, and a green t-shirt is good enough. He calls four times before I leave, checking my estimated time of arrival.

He's dialing my home number again when I walk into the gym, I take two tentative steps toward him, and he's there, pushing me back into the elevator.

On the sidewalk, I fumble with my sunglasses. "Are you going to drive, or should I?"

He takes my hand. "Where are we going?"

Irman flashes white teeth at me. All I can see are incisors. "Pipe down, smart ass. You'll know when we get there."

We cross the street and enter a model apartment, one of presumably many in the new condominium building. "Where are we going?" I ask again, but he holds a finger to his lips as if I'd wake someone.

The main room is white and empty. Irman grabs me around the waist and wrestles me to the perfectly groomed shag carpet. Before we've exchanged thoughts, talked or bartered, he's pulling off his shirt, producing condoms from his socks.

"Can we take this a bit slower?" I say, holding his hand away from my hip.

He smiles like a viper and slides his hands around to cup my ass. "Slow enough?"

His mouth yearns toward my neck. Then he's all over me, grabbing, kissing, pushing me down. Items of clothing fall around us as he forces his way between my legs. I arch my back, trying to use the carpet's texture to make it more sensual. "Wait," I whisper.

"C'mon, you're not going to tease me, are you?"

Then he's inside me. It lasts about six minutes on the long side.

I stare at the ceiling in disbelief when he rolls off me, panting like an overheated engine on an unforgiving day.

Irman stands up immediately after he comes, and I get my first real glance at his body. He's tanned and firm. His abs making Rodin-like ripples. "Wow," I say, admiring him.

He grabs the tiny roll of fat at his midsection, illuminating his only physical imperfection, and turns to the window and the sun outside. I notice the Playboy bunny silhouette tattooed on his left bicep. It mocks me from across the room, and I glance away in embarrassment. The kitchens in these things are pretty small. If I moved in, I would definitely replace the fake brick.

Irman sits, his back against the wall, legs straight out in front of him. I sit on top of him, knees astride his thighs. He fingers the pendant resting between my breasts. "I went to jail once." He ignores my eyes as he turns the green glass over and over.

"Yeah?" I've always thought that telling intimate secrets after sex was like using a Band-aid when a tourniquet was required. Inappropriate.

The least he can do is look me in the eye as he spills his guts. It's spooky watching him converse with my torso. "I was drinking. I was drunk, and I got in this fight with a cop."

I'm astonished by his stupidity, drunk or not. "A cop?"

"Yeah, they sent me up for a year." His hands move to the small of my back and hold me there. I can feel the blood moving through his fingers. "I'm sober now," he says. "Four years."

I make a note, to never give this man my address. "Good for you," I say, trying to sound encouraging.

Confession time is over soon. "I have to get back to work," he says, pushing me off.

I touch his arm, feeling embarrassed and weirdly close to him. "Relax," I joke, as I pull my shorts on over the tights.

He watches me, his expression shifting. I expect it to become hard, professional, like when he watches himself in the mirror. As if this look would allow him to become part of the chrome railings and the harsh overhead light of the club. Instead, his brow wrinkles between his eyes. All I read is sadness.

Playfully, I try to poke and tickle him. He dodges away.

"What are you, married or something?"

He hangs his head. "Yes."

There's a moment of suspended time, and I guess he's waiting for me to slap his face or something. But I throw back my head and a laugh explodes out. Little tears run from the edges of my eyes.

"What's so funny?"

"This," I answer, sweeping the room with my gaze and resting finally on his face.

He holds me, making me look straight at him. "I'm glad you think so. My wife would kill me if she knew."

"If you're unhappy, then why do you stay married?"

"Sometimes I want to be married, and sometimes I don't."

"Okay," I say, sarcasm tingeing my voice.

He kisses me once and we leave by separate exits, adding unnecessary intrigue to the proceedings. I walk back to the gym alone and work up a sweat, like the one I never got around to an hour ago. The weight of the bicycle between my legs feels more solid and forgiving than he was.

The forgettable sex has mostly been forgotten by Monday, when my next shift begins. There's a weird guy who's been calling every day, asking to speak to a new reader each time. He says his name is John, Jerry, Jack or Joseph, and always asks the same question. Today, I get him.

"Hi, my name is Bronwyn. How can I help you today?"

"Yeah, I need to ask about a girl I was going out with. Is she trying to—"

"I have to get some information before I can answer your question. Let's start with your first name and birth date, please."

"John, July 18, 1961."

I note it down on my call sheet. "All right, you were saying you wanted to ask about a girl?"

"Yeah, I was going out with this girl named Robin, and then I thought she was cheating on me, so I broke it off." I can hear the drawn-out *aw* sounds of New York in his voice, and feel a warm welling in my belly.

"Do you want to see if you'll get back together?"

"Well, every few days, someone calls and leaves this weird message on my answering machine saying 'stop it stop it stop it.'" His voices drops into a whisper at the last bit.

I, too, would be creeped out. No doubt about it.

"I want to see if it's her calling."

I shuffle the cards and snap them onto the desk. Queen, queen, then—*whoa*—swords, swords and more swords. A three and a five. A seven, then the Moon.

"You and this person have a lot of karma from past lives, and this may be what's brought you together in this lifetime. But your karma isn't meant to be worked out through a romantic relationship this time around." I'm trying to help, but feel that his energy isn't focused.

"Is it her, though?"

"I don't think it's her. She may be having someone else doing the calling, but if she's calling at all, it's because of something you're doing."

"I'm not doing anything! I swear!"

"You haven't called her?"

"I called her once or twice, and told her to bring back my shit."

"You never went over to her place, or where she works?"

"Well, maybe I did that a couple of times."

"These messages you're receiving have to do with that. She's trying to get you to stop harassing her, so she can move on."

"So you don't think we'll get back together?"

"There's a bit of abuse here. Did either one of you hit the other in your relationship?"

"Sometimes, when we were drunk. But it was only a few times."

"Yeah, unless that's cleared up, I don't see it really working out for you two. Sorry."

Silence.

"Did you want to ask about something else?"

"I want to know who's calling me, so yeah, you could ask about that."

Not sure why that matters, but OK. I lay down a few more cards. Four of Cups—an illusion. I'm not even sure if this is actually happening, or all in this guy's mind.

"The cards are saying that it doesn't really matter who's calling. She's either doing it herself, or having someone do it to scare you off."

"I knew it was her! That bitch!"

Sometimes, I'm learning, it's best to not say what you see, lest someone get the crap beaten out of them unnecessarily.

"Like I said, John. The universe is asking you to move on from this now. The calls will stop soon enough, and then you can meet someone new. Do you want me to ask about that now?"

"No, that fuckin' bitch is gonna pay." He hangs up.

I total my hold time. When I turn around, Katie's standing behind me. "You get that John, Jerry, Joseph guy, too? He's completely nuts."

"Yeah, it seems that way."

"You know, everyone else just combines their hold times into one bigger one. That way, you won't get in trouble from the Boss Man."

"Are you kidding? So everyone lies?"

"Pretty much."

"OK, but I think I'll stick with this method for now."

"Hey, I drew you this picture." She holds out a pencil drawing of a guy standing at microphone, singing into it. He's got mouse ears and a wedge of cheese at his feet. A banner with *Eddie Cheddar* hangs over his head. "You said you weren't a Pearl Jam fan, so . . ."

I laugh, grateful for the image, her sense of humor and camaraderie in this madhouse. "I'm gonna hang it right here, in a place of honor," I say, borrowing a push-pin from the bulletin board and positioning it in front of me on the cubicle wall.

"I think I'm gonna add John, Jerry, Joseph to the Psychic Junkie List." She holds up a notebook she's been drawing in. Only the top part is finished so far. It depicts a fat, slovenly customer, with a phone in his hand and signs of addiction all around; crushed beer cans, hypodermic needles, potato chip bags and other garbage. There are x's in the guy's eyes, and broken hearts all around. He's out of it, too far gone to hear the voices of assistance.

In one image, she's captured how we see our callers. Alone, complacent, unwilling or unable to get up off their asses and do much of anything to stop their own suffering. I laugh, wincing. It's easy to make fun of the lost, much harder to do anything about them.

The shift is soon over, and six of us gather for Martin's first astrology class. I have been borrowing books from the library or driving to the Bodhi Tree's used section to spend my meager discretionary income, and speed-reading them, anxious to fill in the gaps of my knowledge.

Katie and I look at each other as Martin leads us through the first lessons, about the signs and the houses. We try to keep it down, because a new set of readers is taking calls in the same room, but when Martin has to excuse himself to take a call himself, I can't help but laugh.

Katie pushes a note at me that says, "He's like fucking Spock." And it's true. Martin's idea of teaching is to lecture, in a monotone, about the various aspects of the zodiac, illustrating only rarely. When one of us raises a hand to clarify, he furrows his brow in exasperation, or turns an almost scientific eye on us, as if we were lab specimens.

I'm still giggling when he comes back into the room and asks, "Does anyone have any questions?"

We all look at each other, too scared to do anything about our ignorance.

"Good," he says. "Study the handouts and we'll get into aspects and transits next week."

I pack up my things and head out the door. It's still afternoon, and there's still a lot more trouble to get into, if I really try.

I begin to measure time by Irman's calls, which arrive at a frequency of four or five a day. Eventually, I stop answering the phone altogether.

Meanwhile, the graffiti war outside has spread to other trees. Additional taggers have entered the fray—my building bears faded signs of blue and yellow paint flecks where some had tried and failed to dominate the palms. Now, the red initials and the white, two-eye design faced each other from their separate, turfed-out trees, glaring across the expanse like Clint Eastwood on a desert day. Someone's going to reap the whirlwind; it was just a matter of time.

I am on an exercise bike, wearing my headphones cranked to a brain-bending din, when I see Irman again. The elevator door slides open and I can see him leading a wide-eyed, older woman to the counter.

One side of the cassette ends; I wait for it to flip over.

"I want you to meet my wife," Irman says to a trainer behind the counter. His posture is different, slouched, and he doesn't finger his hair at all. His whole bearing is somehow made insignificant by her presence. His wife stands at his side, silent as a monolith.

For me, there's no jealousy, just the cold, hard eye of an observer. Later, I think about food under the direct, hot nozzle of the shower.

Two days later, the wife's picture appears on the virgin terrain of Irman's desk. She looks younger in the photograph, with baby's breath wreathing her face. Her expression is exuberant and hopeful, filled with untold promises. I can see why he's married her, but am unable to resist the temptation. "Feeling guilty?" I chirp as I pass his desk.

Judging from the look he gives me, he wouldn't think twice about hurling a wrench at me, if one had been conveniently lying around.

That should be the last nail, I think. An appropriate ending to an absurd situation. But as I'm leaving the gym, he worms into the elevator behind another passenger. We're almost at the parking garage when he murmurs, "Why haven't you called me back?"

I deploy a laugh, meant to disarm him, then try to walk off with the other passenger when the doors open.

"Wait," he says, in a choked, pathetic whimper.

I hesitate, just for a second, and he turns me around, twisting my arm behind my back. He shoves me back into the elevator and hits the button with his index finger. Out comes a tiny silver key. He locks us between floors, then lifts me up by the waist. I feel small and insignificant in his bodybuilder's grasp. He slams me against the wall and holds me there.

"Lame," I say.

He grabs me around the shoulders, gathering fistfuls of my hair in both of his hands, yanking it until my head jerks back. He bites hard on my neck. I imagine his incisors sinking into my white flesh. "I know what you want," he murmurs. "You like it hard, don't you?"

I feel a scream rising inside. As calmly as possible, I reply, "You're hurting me."

His back rises and falls as he laughs. "You don't know what you're doing to me."

"I'm trying to get my car out of the garage. Is that having a great effect on you?" I struggle to be free of his hands, but I'm pinned like a Van Gogh reproduction on a dorm room wall.

Slowly, his grip loosens; he allows me to drop to the floor. He sinks to his knees, clamping my legs tight together. "You're all I can think about for eighteen whole days."

"Fucking me in some elevator?"

"No, you. Us."

"There is no us. You're married and that's it," I say.

He looks up at me. "Please?"

"Sorry, but I don't do hopeless situations."

"Maybe we could go out sometime."

His voice echoes unanswered in my ears. For a few seconds, I imagine myself out on a date with him, doing the flowers and candy thing, but can't sustain it. The picture in my mind won't last more than five seconds before it disappears in the haze of other thoughts.

"Lose my number, OK?"

I try to push his arms from my legs, but they hold on. In frustration, I turn my head to the wall and rest my nose against the cool tile. Quiet resounds around us.

I jump when he speaks my name.

"Do you miss me?"

"No," I say. Already, I can feel his grasp relenting. I make a mental note to drive past the YWCA on the way home. Maybe they're having a membership sale. I'll join up right away and cancel what I have here. This experiment, fucking what's merely beautiful, is officially a failure.

He wants to know where I've been, who I've been seeing, and what I'm doing later that week. He wants to make plans for the future, plot schedules, and tie me down. I imagine that he sees his tag on me, some spray-paint assertion. After all, he's lived in Los Angeles all his life, and knows a palm tree when he sees one.

November

✯ Scorpio ✯

I am horned out.

Within a few weeks, my vocabulary has expanded with words like quincunx and immum coeli. I care, more than I have cared about anything else in recent memory, to stuff my head with all kinds of this ancient knowledge. I spend perilous amounts of money, often cutting into my grocery budget, on books about tarot, astrology and mythology. I read Robert Graves, Suzuki Roshi, Starhawk and Barbara Marciniak.

When I'm not working, I read. I read in line at the post office, in my car, at stoplights, on the treadmill at the gym. I read before bed, while I'm eating dinner, before the movie starts when I'm waiting for a friend to arrive. I think of all the people who have come before me, around the globe, all of them seekers. When I was younger, the more I tried to learn, the more I was shushed and told to smile. When my brain yearned for stimulation, I got furrowed brows and annoyed silences. My questions hung in the air between my teachers and me, my family and me, hell, between almost anyone and me. I have always been too curious for my own good.

Each shift at Astral Planet becomes a new opportunity to learn. Though sometimes I go home drained and sick of talking, I arrive at work excited to talk to my new friends. Many of them don't share my enthusiasm, but they're involved in these fields more than anyone I've ever met. It's like an enormous living library from which to borrow. And I'm definitely here to borrow.

The main problem is that my salary isn't cutting it. One morning, I sit down to write out my bills, and quickly realize my salary won't cover them. I can pay my rent late, but don't relish another call from Homer, my landlord. I can try to get more shifts, but they're so underpaid that I'm not sure it would work out that way, either.

Something needs to give. A few minutes after I have that thought, I get a call from Opal. I answer the phone, looking guiltily at the stack of books on the floor by the couch.

"Hey! I'm so bored! What are you doing?"

I try not to exhale, but it comes out anyway. "Writing out bills."

"Don't do that! Come out with me!" Opal never speaks without a lot of emphasis. In fact, she's so squirmy at AstralPlanet that she's gotten in trouble more than once for talking too loud, laughing too loud, and just generally being a spazz. She gets on some people's nerves, but I think she's funny. I don't have to live with her.

"What are you doing?"

"I'm going around to all these places, trying to see if these places will let me read cards. You want to come with me?"

"Absolutely!" And before I'm even aware of what the Law of Attraction is, here it comes, barreling into my life.

"Great! I'm coming over right now!"

I have no idea if I've even told her my address, but she's pounding on my door around twenty minutes later, yelling my name in the hall.

Opal drives like she talks, veering from one lane into the other without signaling, and yelling out the window whenever she sees a cute guy, which is pretty damn often.

I'm used to the decidedly unique styles of New York taxi drivers, but my stomach isn't ready for a drive from Venice to West Hollywood with Opal. She screeches into a Starbucks and gets some coffee, which scares me. Luckily, I can't stand even the smell of coffee, so my mellow won't be harshed. Once she gets the caffeine into her system, though, she unexpectedly calms down. At least I feel safe enough to let go of the door handle, and notice fingernail marks above my knees, where I've been digging them in. Not cute for making a first impression, but that's the way it is. Neither of us is going to win any prizes in that department, anyway.

We start out at a new teahouse on West 3rd Street, and I mistakenly let her do the talking. "Hey, Mister Man. We're tarot reading weirdos, and we're looking for work. How would you like us to read some of your customers, and get them to order more tea from you?"

A vaguely distasteful look crosses his face, barely discernible. "We're not really looking for anything like that now."

Unwisely, she presses on. "C'mon, man. We're really good. You want us to give you a reading now?"

"No." I can see the curtain come down on his face, and now he just wants us gone.

I tug on Opal's arm. "Thanks," I say to him over my shoulder as we make our way out to the street.

"I could have gotten him to let us do it!"

"I don't think so, buddy."

"You're my buddy! You're my buddy!" She dances around on the sidewalk, throwing her arms around my neck and hugging me fiercely. It's like being mauled by a big, upright puppy.

We try four other places, with similar results.

"I have no money!" she tells one woman. "You have to hire us or we'll starve."

Maybe not the best sales tactic, and it doesn't work anyway. As the sun sinks into an orange sky, I've actually spent money, on juice, tea and water, and made none.

God damn it.

I have no idea how I'm going to make ends meet, this month or any other. But I know Opal's idea probably isn't going to fly. Maybe we're too strange for them, or they think we'll put a spell on them or something. The bottom line is I need to find some better work soon.

I've had eight years of editorial experience in New York, so I update my resume when I get home, using my wheezing dot matrix printer to spit out cover letters and labels to a few local possibilities. There's not much publishing here, but maybe my years in film production back east will make a good impression. Even some part-time work would help.

By the time I'm hungry for dinner, I realize I have no food, nothing to create a real meal. I eat a few crackers with mustard while digging in my desk for some stamps, but it's just not going to assuage the hunger. I've got maybe eight bucks in my pocket, and another four or five bucks in change lying around. Wouldn't a real psychic just be able to choose five or six numbers, win the lottery, and retire young?

I earmark one of my dollars for this purpose and silently ask the universe for help. It'll be hard to read anybody's cards if I don't have anywhere to live.

On the way downstairs, I remember I haven't gotten my mail, so I stick my key in and a slew of envelopes, bills, newspapers and postcards slide out. Guess I've kind of forgotten to pick it up for a few days. I'm standing there, trying to get it into a manageable pile, when I hear a male voice behind me.

"Anything good in there?"

I turn. He's tall and dark, with warm hazel eyes standing out against brown hair. I'm guessing Italian ancestry, maybe just south of the border with Switzerland. "I'm not sure yet," I say, smiling.

"Oh, you're in 9. I guess Fish moved out."

"Yeah, but I kept his door."

"Isn't that the best?"

"Yeah, I couldn't bring myself to have it painted over."

"Good for you! I'm Kevin," he says, sticking out his hand.

"Alyson." He looks to be a few years younger than I am, but not much too much. I'm terrible at judging people's ages, anyway. He could be ten years older, and I'd be none the wiser.

"Well, I'll be seeing you around, Alyson. Maybe sooner than later."

Oh my God, is he flirting with me?

"See ya!" I call, watching his back disappear down the stairs.

Mmmmmm. He's full of possibilities.

Katie's got her Ouija board out when I arrive the next morning. She and Patrice are sitting knee to knee, and something about the way that Patrice is holding her body suggests more than just a passing interest in channeling. The planchette slips across the board, lighter than air, as the spirits spell out words.

I put my books down on my desk and sit, rapt, as Katie receives this information. I don't even know what they're asking about, but the sight of this divine communication is pretty cool to watch up close. Patrice has her fingers tented on the planchette, too, and when it comes to a stop, she pauses to write down the letters they've been given.

Katie opens her eyes and seems to come back to the waking world. "Hi," she says drowsily, realizing I've arrived for work. "That was deep."

Patrice tallies the letters into words, then begins to read aloud, "Work has been especially impressive lately. Blue will now be a color you cushion your elemental structure with."

I catch myself internally wanting to edit the sentence for grammar.

Katie laughs. "Blue?" None of us is wearing the color.

Patrice continues, "Alyson will now come to many astrological levels of information, where she will need to practice wise judgment. Now, you enter the level of refined astrology, where you need to feel the elements and practice judgment. You will make the jump and claim glory. What do you fancy hearing?"

Katie turns to me, a smile of amazement on her face. "I guess they knew you were coming."

I've just started learning astrology, the part beyond the Sun Sign in the newspaper, at least. I have no idea what they're talking about. But it's sort of thrilling to be talked about in that way, by strangers no less, invisible strangers who're talking about me. Bizarre.

Katie asks, "You want to try?"

I'm dying to, but part of me is embarrassed. What if I suck at it, in front of all these professionals?

"Maybe in a minute," I answer. "I'd like to watch you do it a little longer."

They move together again, knees touching. Patrice reaches out to run a wisp of Katie's hair back behind her ear. It's almost maternal, but charged with sexuality all the same.

Katie sinks back into the trance, closing her eyes and seeming to lose consciousness, very slowly. Her head droops forward, her eyelids flutter, but her hands shoot out, following the plastic triangle around the board. This time, it jerks up and down, making a jagged path around the board, to its final destination.

Patrice transcribes quickly. "You will need to carve away the inappropriate layerings that create a lovely, cozy image. You will need to extract the essential. Alyson, you are clear and right. You will benefit from practicing the information you just got."

Katie snaps her eyes open and stares right at me. "What did you see in your mind right now? They want you to hold onto that. It's the direction you need to go in now."

I shrug, unable to hold onto anything I see. Just the same, I feel tears welling behind my eyes, though I don't know why. For the first time in my life, I can feel that someone, or something, is looking out for me. Some larger energy force cares enough to talk to me through a child's board game. I feel strangely enveloped with love.

All I can see in my mind is the ocean, beating against the shore, relentlessly.

I laugh, trying to cover, shrugging again.

Katie keeps her gaze on me. "You'll remember it in dreams. Ask them to show it to you."

I sign on and take a few calls, while they channel quietly in the corner. Patrice has had some trouble with a lover, and wants to determine the best path of action. Seems these questions are not confined to the callers.

The first one is a young kid, judging by the sound of his voice.

"Is this the psychic?"

"Yeah, what's your name?"

"You sound more like a psycho!" he screams. I catch a snatch of laughter before the phone slams down.

Name? I make it up. Hold time? 1 minute.

The second call is an older woman. "I'd like to get a reading, please."

"Sure, I just have to get your first name . . ."

"Velma."

"And your date of birth."

"June 9, 1942."

"All right, then, what can I help you with today?"

"Could you please give me the lottery numbers for this week?"

I suppose it's a fair question, but for some reason it floors me. You're spending five bucks a minute for a person who hasn't won the lottery before (hence the job) to tell you how to do it.

"Um, let me just put you on hold for one second . . ."

I turn to Mercy, who's staring at the ceiling tiles. "This lady is asking about the lottery numbers. I have no idea how to do that."

Lazily, she says, "Just pick five numbers."

"Really? I don't know if I can do that in good faith."

She pushes herself into an upright position. "All right, I'll do it."

She transfers the woman back to her extension and reads five numbers out of the air. "Yes, ma'am. It's 5, 8, 13, 45 and 51. Yes, that's right. Good luck, now."

Mercy bends over her time sheet, updating.

"Does that happen a lot?" I ask.

"All the time," she says, in a bored tone of voice.

"If it's all the same to you, can I not do those calls? It just . . . isn't right."

She looks at me like a foundling in the woods, like a holy innocent. The sarcasm dripping off her is palpable. "If you say so. I can use the minutes."

When Mercy takes a break later that afternoon, Katie talks me into trying out the Ouija board. I feel a little safer, now that Patrice has packed it in for the day. Though she can be really funny, her obsession with Katie can be a little territorial, and I don't want to get in the middle of that. Not in my workplace. Not for a million bucks.

"I'll receive, and you ground," she tells me.

"What does that mean?"

"Well, I'm going to go out there and get the information, and you stay here and make sure we're connected to the earth. Make sense?"

"I think so?"

She levels her gaze at me, no bullshit. "You know what you're doing. Now all you have to do is do it. When I tell you the letters, just write them down."

We put our fingertips on the planchette, and it immediately takes off, dusting my fingers and leaving them tumbling around on the board. I manage to catch up—Katie is, by now, wearing an expression of impatience—and mount the planchette again;

it zips off. I soon figure out how to keep my fingertips strongly attached to it without weighing it down. What's weirdest about it is that it feels like it's literally floating a quarter of an inch off the surface of the board, not scraping along its surface.

The neat-o aspect is hard to ignore, but I have a job to do. I imagine myself pinned to the ground, as if my feet are the roots of a tree, gnarled and dark. I see these roots plunging into the soil, reaching down to the core of the earth. With part of my attention, I keep us there, and with the other, I write.

"M-A-N-I-F-E-S-T-I-N-G-I-S-A-U-N-I-O-N-T-H-E-O-T-H-E-R-E-N-E-R-G-Y-M-U-S-T-B-E-C-O-N-S-I-D-E-R-E-D."

"Manifesting is a union. The other energy must be considered," I read.

Katie continues. "B-O-T-H-P-A-R-T-I-E-S-M-U-S-T-B-E-I-N-V-O-L-V-E-D-A-LY-S-O-N-W-I-L-L-F-I-N-D-A-P-L-A-C-E-T-H-A-T-S-E-R-V-E-S-H-E-R-N-E-E-D-S-E-F-F-I-C-I-E-N-T-L-Y."

"Both parties must be involved. Alyson will find a place that serves her needs efficiently."

Katie's face changes, becoming more concentrated. "A-L-Y-S-O-N-P-A-T-I-E-N-C-E-I-S-O-N-E-O-F-T-H-E-V-I-R-T-U-E-S-Y-O-U-W-I-L-L-A-C-Q-U-I-R-E-H-E-R-E."

"Alyson, patience is one of the virtues you will acquire here." I want to laugh out loud at that one. Patience has never been one of my strong suits.

"T-H-E-P-A-T-H-Y-O-U-A-R-E-O-N-I-S-B-E-I-N-G-R-E-V-E-A-L-E-D-O-N-E-S-T-E-P-A-T-A-T-I-M-E-F-O-R-G-O-O-D-R-E-A-S-O-N-I-F-Y-O-U-R-U-N-O-U-T-O-F-M-O-N-E-Y-I-T-I-S-T-O-M-O-V-E-Y-O-U-I-N-A-P-A-R-T-I-C-U-L-A-R-D-I-R-E-C-T-I-O-N."

"The path you are on is being revealed one step at a time. For good reason, if you run out of money, it is to move you in a particular direction."

Katie comes out of the trance, seeming to blossom into it like a flower. "Man, they were really wanting you to hear that last bit. There's something about money that's going to send you in a completely new direction."

Sounds like the story of my life, but I don't know her well enough to tell her that yet.

Katie yawns, stretches and gets up for a minute, placing the board on her desk. This is all just another few minutes of another day to her. But I want more.

"Can I try?"

"You mean receiving?'

"Yeah."

"You think you can handle it?" She's teasing, but I can still feel the sting of wanting to fit in, to do well.

"I have no idea what I'm doing. I just want to try."

We switch seats, though I have no idea why that matters. Mercy slouches back into the room, trailing cigarette smoke and slugging from a huge paper cup of coffee.

"Are you corrupting her?" This is directed at Katie.

"I certainly hope so."

Katie winks at me. "Try to extend yourself all the way into the sky. Just send your energy out there and see what comes back. Don't worry about being right."

"Can I try to see if I can channel someone who's dead?"

"Sure."

"I want to channel Carson McCullers." I have no idea why I even say that. I've just been reading her short stories and have fallen in love with the prose.

"Who's that?"

"She's a writer. You know, *A Member of the Wedding*? *Ballad of the Sad Café*? Never mind."

"Whatever, dude. It's your funeral."

The last thing I remember is trying to make sure I wasn't hogging the planchette, and making room for Katie's fingers to rest there. I saw it move a little, jerking at first, and then shooting almost off the board.

Then Katie is shaking me by the shoulder. "Hey, you all right? Alyson?"

I am swooning, hot around the cheeks. "It's boiling in here," I slur.

"Shit." Katie gets up, goes to the water cooler in the hallway, and brings me back a cup of cold water. I drink it down in one gulp.

"What the fuck?"

"You passed out or something. You were talking funny, kind of drawling in a Southern accent."

"What did I say?" I'm embarrassed to admit that I don't know, and kind of weirded out to have lost control like that in front of people I don't know all that well. Even Mercy is watching me with wide eyes, leaned at the edge of the desk with a folded newspaper in her hand. She's been fanning me with it for the past few minutes.

Katie turns to the notebook she's been scribbling in. "You stopped calling out letters a few seconds into it, and just started talking. This is what you said: 'Alyson has always been fiercely independent. She must be led slowly to the people she will work with, or she will run. Alyson, your volatile nature must be preserved, yet cooperation will be required. Alyson's mission is unique. She needs to develop a new approach. She needs to submit her ideas to backers. She must not be judgmental about money holders. All are similar.'"

I feel a chill run down the back of my neck when she reads this. Part of it feels so familiar, as if I really did say it. I haven't told Katie about some of the bigger ideas I've had recently, creative ideas about films and books and possibly theater pieces. I haven't even told some of my closest friends about these ideas, because they seem so grandiose and undoable now.

Katie, scanning my expression, can see that this has rung a bell. "It's like you're there and not there, isn't it? Like you're way back at the very top of the bleachers, listening in on a conversation a thousand miles away."

"Yeah, that's what it feels like." I'm still in a complete daze, and remember at least I don't have to drive myself home any time soon. Maybe some caffeine.

"She said one more thing: 'Tell her she'll still be young and fuckable, baby.'" Then she's laughing, and Mercy's laughing, and Martin comes into the room then and I want to laugh, too, but it's still too close and too real, even though it's not.

Martin stands close to Katie, who looks up at him and coos, "I'm teaching the delicate flower how to channel."

Mercy's twisting in her seat, trying to get Martin's attention. She looks like she has to pee or something. As usual, he has no idea she's even in the room.

"That and the astrology's gonna make you a psychic, no matter what you do." I realize this must be as close as he gets to teasing, though it sounds so threatening, I have to concentrate hard not to screw my face into an ugly look. He grins at me, looking anal and almost rictus-y, then leaves the room. Katie rolls her eyes at me.

"Her energy was so slow and heavy," I say.

"I know. They're all completely different. But for a first time, that was pretty incredible."

By the time I get home, I'm completely beat. All afternoon, it's been hard to concentrate in the wake of my first channeling session. I can't decide if I'm a genius, for getting it on the first try, or a complete failure, who can't even keep it together like Patrice and Katie. Maybe all I am is tired now, sick of helping the lovelorn when all I want is a beer.

I'm carrying a backpack full of books and notes in one hand, and two plastic grocery bags in the other when I see something taped to the door of my apartment.

A pang of horror shoots me—did I remember to pay the rent? Fuck!

Wait, yeah I paid it. About a week ago. *Phew.*

Then a surge of curiosity comes. I get to the door, and find a note there, written in huge blocky letters: Come find me when you get home—basement apartment next to the laundry room. Want to go get a drink?—Kevin.

After a quick shower, I change into a simple black dress and a jean jacket with the ever-present boots. I have no "real" female shoes, save for a few pairs of thrift store finds in dubious condition. A few swipes of makeup, and it's on.

Smoke pours from Kevin's apartment when he opens the door, and his slitty eyes are all I need to see. "Neighbor!" he exclaims. "Pretty neighbor!"

I can see that he's about to stumble forward and give me a hug, then he thinks better of it.

"Looks like somebody got the party started without me."

"Don't come in here! I mean, I would invite you in, but it's a fucking mess, and I haven't had time to clean. I just got off work."

"Me too!"

"Really? What do you do?" He's grabbing a leather jacket off a chair stacked with records, clothes, and unopened mail, from the looks of it.

Let's see—what do I do? "Um, I'm a counselor," I say, finally.

"Oh, like a shrink?"

"Kind of, but without all the degrees and whatnot."

"We may need your skills before the night is over," he says, mysteriously.

"What do you do?"

He takes my hand and leads me out into the chilly blue night of Venice.

There's a bar not far from our building, down two blocks and in one, which I'd have never found on my own. It's hiding behind a tall curtain of bamboo plants and looks more like a supper club than a bar. We take a seat and get drinks, which he insists on paying for.

"The least I can do for pretty neighbor," he beams.

Turns out he's been working on the new Johnny Depp movie, technically a PA but more like a personal assistant. Johnny's nice, he says, and hysterical in a very low-key way. He's having his Winona Forever tattoo removed one letter at a time, and now it reads Wino Forever.

We talk for around an hour. He's very engaging company, pays for all the drinks, and it begins to feel like a date, except he's not really making a move. Instead, he treats me with a kind of courtly distance that's charming but confusing. I don't know if this guy is my brother, or somebody interested in a little more.

A few drinks later, he touches my hand, very lightly, and says it's been a great night. "I could tell you were an interesting person," he says. "You've just got that look about you. You're not like everyone else."

"Well, yeah, thanks. And thanks for the drinks. It's great to meet you and hang out and everything." I stop short of saying "we should do it again sometime," not wanting to misread the signals. I am so fucking bad at this.

We walk back to our building in a kind of cool mist coming off the water, two blocks away. It's like moving through a dream, so romantic. He puts his arm around my shoulder as we get closer to home, and kisses me sweetly on the cheek before bidding me goodnight.

I don't want sweet, damn it.

All night I toss and turn, under unforgiving covers that don't come close to resembling the reassuring weight of a human body beside me.

The next day, I have to clean out my locker at the gym, because I've found one closer to home, which will let me pay as I go. If I want, I can walk there, to get even more exercise. Irman is furrowed over his desk when I walk in, and I scuttle in, grab the few things I have stored there, and go. Wow, I don't think he saw me. Maybe I've made my point after all.

I suppose I could drop off my card and make it official, but I don't care enough to do that. The elevator's taking way too long, so I dash up the side stairs and run up three flights before he can start any more shit. My car is exactly where I left it and the parking attendant eyes me curiously, wondering about my extremely short workout.

There's a black pickup nearby, and I indicate that I'm about to leave the space, if he wants it. The guy behind the wheel just looks blankly at me, unfocused but looking in my direction. I wave again, no response.

I move to the door of my car and insert my key. He pulls a little closer. But he's still looking right and left like he doesn't realize I'm leaving. So I walk up to the passenger side door of his truck, and lean in a little. "Hey, I'm leaving, if you need a space."

His eyes dart down to his crotch, nervously. His dick is out, no mistaking that. It's long and distended, bright pink with blood. I'm close enough to see the veins along its surface, the individual idiosyncrasies that make it his own.

I flash my eyes back up to his face but it's completely inscrutable. Not leering, not embarrassed. Just looking straight ahead, without expression. He strokes it up and down a little absently, as you would a pet while you're reading the paper. Up and down, up and down.

I back away from the window and move to my car. Why does this seem like the perfect ending? When I pull out onto Pico, the sun is so blinding I feel like my retina are sizzling. For a few seconds, I have no idea where I'm going. My mind is just blank, wiped clean by all I've seen.

What do I need? How do I get it? And when is it going to arrive?

Finally, I decide to stop by the Psychic Eye Bookstore on my way home. It's on Main Street in Santa Monica, close enough to home. My mind is still blank, and I feel like I want to tell someone about the empty-faced guy in the truck, touching himself like I wasn't even there, but I know that's not possible. Instead, I wander through the aisles, throwing supplies into a wire basket. I pick up a few pullout pink candles, both in jars, and a book on candle magic. There's incense, Venus and Mars oils, a CD of meditative music and a Liz Greene book. All I'll need to get this damn masculine-feminine thing sorted out.

They've seen it all before, I'm sure, just like us. At the cash register is a woman who seems to be following a man around the store. He's trying to pay for something, I can't see what from where I'm standing, and urging the clerk on with his eyes.

"Did you think I would just dry up and blow away when you didn't call me, asshole?

The man's eyes flash when she says this. The edges of his mouth tighten, just a little.

"What's the matter? Cat got your tongue? Hard to believe you're at a loss for words. You, of all people."

He extends his hand across the counter to offer the clerk some cash. She's got her head down, trying to be there and not be there at the same time.

I turn, and see the other clerks, and a few readers, watching the fireworks from the incense aisle. One shakes her head and heads back into her curtained off reading area.

The clerk makes change, while the guy's hand hangs in the air between them, waiting for it.

The woman tries to push her body into his sight line, but he's pressed against the counter and she can only angle her hip into him. "You must really think a lot of yourself," she says. "Quite the big man you are. I shouldn't be surprised you turned out to be a self-involved autodidact, though. You have no room for anyone's opinion but your own, do you?"

What the hell is an autodidact?

She tails him as he makes for the door. He hisses, "I never promised you anything, Rita. You have to realize that sometimes, things don't work out. That's all."

She's rocked back on her heels for a second, maybe because he actually addressed her. But she keeps after him until he pushes the door open with both hands and makes his way, head down, into the street. I wonder, and perhaps we all do, if she'll follow him out there, considering she's got a few hundred bucks' worth of merchandise in her hands.

But she stands at the door, with it pushed open in her hands. We can all see she's trying to figure out the cruelest thing she can think of to say to him. We'd all probably do the same. She opens her mouth and time seems to slow down, "You know what, Dan? You have no soul!"

And with that, she slams the door closed as best she can (it's on springs after all) and walks back to the counter as if nothing's happened.

Technically, I'm next in line, but I take a step back to let her through. She slaps her books on the counter and says, "I'm going to take these, but I want to look around a little more."

She walks away, whistling to herself. I put my stuff on the counter and pay with no further drama. On the street, I look around to see if the guy is waiting in the bushes to do away with Rita, former something-or-other in his life.

I wish I knew what the fucking universe is trying to tell me.

For the rest of the evening, I open my candle magic book and find an old Exact-o knife. There are symbols for love, for affection and friendship. There are symbols for planets and flowers and hearts. Some are angular and geometrical, while others take several minutes to carve into the candle wax. I make one for love, putting down all I want to manifest. I describe the kind of guy I want: caring, funny and kind. Someone employed, who's not a psycho or a stalker or a deadbeat. I want someone independent, ambitious and creative. He has to like cool music, movies and traveling. He has to like Thai food and trying new things. He has to get that I sometimes am not an easy person to understand, or live with, or categorize.

Maybe an hour has passed when I feel I've finished that one. I smear it in Venus oil and set it back into the glass jar. The second candle I leave for now. If I need it, I'll carve it. But for now, I believe I can make this happen, and clear away the confusion around me.

Before I light the candle, I say, "Please send someone real. Send me someone who's not crazy, or stalker-y, or unclear. Send someone who could love me."

The sulfur match sounds unnaturally loud in the room when I yank it against the friction surface. But the flame joins the wick and soon it burns down to the surface of the wax. The smell of the Venus oil, flowery and cloying, fills the room. I let it surround me, get into my pores, become me. At this point, I have no idea how to do this on my own.

I don't have a bathtub, so I put the candle on the white tile counter top in the kitchen and get lost in a novel for an hour or so, until my eyes are droopy and tired. In the past, I'd have just slept where I fell, but if I want a real relationship, maybe I have to actually sleep in the bed I'm renting. So I haul myself to the bedroom, carrying the candle with me into the bathroom. The book says you're not supposed to blow the candle out once you've lit it, so I leave it in the bathroom sink, assuming it'll do the least amount of damage there, should anything happen.

The last image in my mind before I fall asleep is a series of waves lapping at the shore, gently yet persistently.

A few hours later, I'm awakened by a loud pop. I spring up in bed, wondering if it's gunfire from nearby Oakwood. But there's another pop, very close, and I can see a column of fire three or four feet high, splashing light out the bathroom door. For a few seconds, it's like a slow-motion dream, the devotional candle, the fire of rebirth, the purification and renewal.

Then I realize the holder can't possibly withstand this, so I bolt out of bed. I get there as the glass breaks in an explosion of shards, and the fire catches the oil along the candle's surface.

"Shit!" I look around frantically, trying to find something I don't mind losing. Finally, I choose a shitty black towel with the consistency of sandpaper. Stupidly, I turn on the faucet, which sends the fire whooshing almost as high as the ceiling. I wrench the tap shut. Oil and water, apparently, don't mix.

I beat the fire out with the towel, using my fingertips to douse the wick when it gets low enough. My heart is thudding hard, as much from the exertion as the fear that I might not be able to put the fire out. When it's over, the sink is singed with black ash and mixed with bright red Venus oil. It looks like some sort of blood sacrifice has taken place.

I sweep the shards of glass up with the towel, and dump them into the garbage can. Maybe I can salvage part of the candle, but it's now burned on all sides, looking more like an experiment gone wrong than a magical ritual. I can read some of the words and symbols I spent so long carving, but most are melted into an indecipherable mess. The largest shard of glass has an imprint of a heart on it, and a thin black line of soot severing it in two.

What is *that* supposed to mean?

The next morning, I'm exhausted. It's not been easy falling back asleep when your home has almost burned down because of your own stupidity. My mind is racing and active, but my body is heavy and tired. Food is the last thing on my mind, but I have to eat if I'm going to get through this day. I have to have caffeine as well, and hope I've had the self-preservation to arrange for some diet soda in the fridge.

Thankfully, there's half a can of very flat Diet Dr. Pepper there. I can't face food now, and when I pad back into the bathroom to wash my face, I have to deal with the war zone of the sink. It actually looks worse, now that the ash has settled into the grooves in the porcelain and the oil has morphed into a pinkish, inner organ kind of color. Ugh. My head is killing me.

I fumble around under the sink and find some cleanser, then scrub the crap out of it until most of the color comes up. This is going to take more than one cleaning, I can tell. But at least I'm able to wash my face and get a little moisturizer on, until I'm almost self-respecting.

Checking the clock, I realize I have to meet Opal, her ex-husband and new boyfriend for brunch in forty-five minutes. In West Hollywood. So I dress quickly, pulling a vintage dress over my head and checking for pit stains and grandma smells before pulling on my boots. Some lipstick, a little mascara, and I'm good to go.

Racing out to the parking lot, I'm digging for my keys when I hear Kevin's voice. The window of his apartment opens onto the parking lot, but he's not talking to me. There's a skinny blond, a model type, clomping around in his sneakers, tripping and cursing and smoking a cigarette.

"God damn it!" she says, tripping again.

I slow down, catching her eye, then looking over to Kevin, who's sitting in the windowsill, looking at her.

"Hey!" he says to me. "This is my neighbor, Alyson. She's really cool."

Nameless Blond Chick with a Distinct Model Vibe shakes my hand with small, moist hands. I can't even hate her. I just have no idea what's going on. "Hey," she says. "I can't seem to stop cursing today."

"Nice to meet you," I say, laughing. I move to the driver's side door, desperate to get the fuck out of there, but he hops out of the window and pads over in his bare feet. He's wide open, friendly and not avoiding me, which is probably what I would do in his shoes.

"Wait, you mentioned you liked jazz, so I made you this tape."

Gingerly, he picks his way across the lot and moves to his car, opens the door and gets a cassette from the glove compartment. Then he hands it to me with a cute little smile.

"Wow, thanks. I'll listen to it now, but I have to meet some friends, so I gotta go."

"All right, let me know what you think."

Fat chance, belly dance. I try not to run anyone over as I back out of my space, but I can't lay rubber fast enough to the freeway.

Do I have a sign on my back that says "fuck with me"?

Am I the queen of mixed messages?

Tears come to my eyes, just for a second, before I shove them back down. Music, that'll help. I pop the tape in and Sonny Rollins' saxophone fills the small space of the car. "My Funny Valentine"—slow and sexy and sad.

Are you kidding?

December
☆ Sagittarius ☆

I am craving adventure.

"What's the first thing you notice about this chart?"

It's Monday again, and we're gathered for another astrology class. Martin is presiding over a small brood of hens, since Aaron dropped out last week. He mostly kept to himself anyway, and rarely contributed to the conversation. But the prevalence of estrogen seems to unnerve Martin, or perhaps excite him. Katie keeps him in a lather anyway, manipulating for all she's worth.

It's practically jumping off the page at me, from the moment I see the chart. "Well, she's got Pluto moving through her eighth house," I say.

"That's right. What does that mean to you?"

"Eighth is the house of transformation and death, and Pluto is the planet of death. Wow, she also had Saturn on her Sun at the time of her death."

He looks at me with that scientific coldness again. I feel like a butterfly pinned to a board. "Very good. Everyone see what she's talking about?"

Patrice wrinkles her nose with derision. "No, can you show me?"

Martin leans over Katie, sitting between them, to show her the eighth house. Katie makes a face at me behind his back.

"See the way Saturn is exactly conjunct the Sun here? And the Progressed Moon is on top of her natal Neptune? Remember, she was delusional. She heard voices. The Neptune is opposing Mercury in the 2nd House."

Katie's face lights up with understanding. "I see! And the Mars in the 10th, the house of the father . . ."

"And the patriarchy."

"And the career," Patrice adds.

"She was a problem for men. They couldn't deal with the way she was."

"Almost like a thorn in their side," he answers.

"But her Saturn was trining the Sun. Couldn't that mean that she was her own authority?"

"Or she took on authority," he says, looking pointedly at me.

"Wait," Katie says, pulling my copy of the chart towards her. "How did you see that?"

"I just did it in my head."

"What are you, some kind of Math Geek?"

I admit it. I like math. Always have, ever since high school. You can count on math; it's always the same, always there for you. Still, it's embarrassing to be called out as a Math Geek in front of everyone. "Fuck off," I say with a smile.

Everyone snickers, and Katie falls silent. Martin seems oblivious, staring at the chart for inspiration. "Everyone see the Jupiter-Uranus trine as well?"

Heads nod all around, though it's hard to tell if we're all on the same page or not.

Martin continues, "Jupiter in the 11th, house of groups and ideals, and then the Uranus in the 3rd, house of communications. She was destined to gather a following, by virtue of her energy and her message. Can you see that?"

Mercy interjects, "I'm really noticing the Scorpio Rising here, and the fixed energy of the Saturn in the 7th. It's so subversive and sexy."

He eyes her like a small child. "But she never had sex, Mercy. It was all subverted for God."

"Oh, yeah, I mean . . . it wasn't real sex, just . . ."

"Imaginary sex?" Katie asks, arching an eyebrow.

Mercy stammers, "No, you know what I mean. It's just . . ."

The phone rings, and she goes to answer it.

"That's enough for today," Martin says, rising from his seat. "I've got to get back to my article anyway."

We murmur thanks as he taps his files on the table and makes his exit. Katie rolls her eyes in Mercy's direction. The new readers are coming on, and I grab my books. "Wait up," Katie calls.

We're almost out the door when she leans in. "You know she has kids."

I drop my voice, "Mercy?"

"Yeah, she had two kids. Boys. But she just left them with some relative when she didn't want to take care of them anymore. Everyone knows."

"I didn't know." There is something horrifying about this knowledge, and the fact that I will never be able to look at her the same way again.

"How old are they?"

"Now? They're probably, like ten and thirteen. But she left them when they were little kids."

"Where are they?"

117

"I don't know."

"Does she see them?"

"I don't think so. But everyone knows. Or, I should say, Martin knows, which is the same thing. He's sooner fuck a tree trunk than spend the night with her. But she'll never give up."

"How did everyone find out?"

"There was one night we were all out together and she was all over Martin, drunk. He went home, to be with this woman he was dating, and she told us."

Man, I wish she hadn't told me that. Now I won't be able to shake that off. I see a coldness in Katie I've never seen before.

Maybe this is how it is, when you can see things no one else does. Maybe it makes you into a kind of warrior, with a deeper love of the spiritual than the corporeal. Maybe love is like that, too, requiring the kind of armor I just don't seem to possess.

Later, I meet up with Felicity and Freddie at Hamburger Hamlet in Century City, perched among some of the only tall buildings in Los Angeles. It looks really familiar until someone mentions that they shot part of *Die Hard* there. Can't say I remember much of that movie.

Felicity's at the bar, already into her second vodka, when I arrive. She's looking well, and a lot happier than the last time I saw her. Sleeping on someone's shitty pullout futon couch probably has that effect on most people. Freddie's behind the bar, loading a waitress' tray with drinks, wiping down the bar at the other end, beaming at an older woman in a leopard print blouse, drinking alone.

Then he's standing in front of me. "Hey, what can I get you, stranger?"

"Stoli-cranberry, I guess." I'm hoping he's not mad that Felicity came to my house to recuperate from their falling out. I don't want to get in the middle of anything.

He sticks a plastic straw in his mouth and goes to prepare my drink. I turn to Felicity. "Looks like you two are getting along."

"Yeah, everything's fine," she says. "We're thinking about whether it would be a good idea or not to have a baby."

The idea sends a stabbing feeling through my heart. I can't imagine anyone I know having the wherewithal to care for an infant, even though most of us are thirty or above now. Most of us have subsistence jobs, and look for the cheapest places to buy life's essentials. Maybe that's how it's done. I have no real idea. People tell me there is no good time to have a child. You just do it.

"Wow, that's a big decision."

"Yeah, but we might just go make a movie instead." I try not to laugh.

A few hours and several drinks later, Freddie's friend Bob comes out of the kitchen, where he works, to have a drink at the end of his shift. He sits on the other side of Felicity, but he and I are soon talking over her, mostly about music. Turns out he plays a little, and wants to get a band together. Leave it to me, and I will find the only musician in the room. In fact, count on it.

"Have you been to any shows since you've been here?" he asks.

"One or two, but I'm still finding my way around."

"Oh, man. We should go out sometime, see some music."

Did he just ask me out?

"Sure, yeah. Maybe I should give you my number." I scribble it on a bar mat and he shoves it deep into his back pocket before shambling out.

"You're flirting with him," Felicity teases.

"Maybe . . ."

Freddie comes over to make sure we've got fresh drinks, but by then I can tell I'm going to have to switch to water, or drive home drunk—not a good idea. Felicity says, "Bob likes Alyson. He just asked her out."

"Really? I'll have to give him some shit. Just be careful. That guy is weird."

"Really? Weird how?"

"I don't know. Just weird."

"I thought he was a friend of yours."

"Yeah, sort of, but I'm telling you, there's just something strange about that dude."

Bob calls me twice, leaving messages both times, before we finally hook up by phone, around a week later. "I've been wondering if you were serious, about going out to see a band sometime," he says.

"Oh, sure. Yeah. I mean, I don't know many of the local bands, so that would be cool. Or just anything, really. I just don't know that many people who care about music like I do."

"Freddie said you were in a band?"

I laugh, unprepared for this line of questioning. "Um, well, I was in a band for maybe fifteen minutes, in New York. We were called Kitten, and I was either kicked out of the band, or left of my own accord—it depends on who you ask. I just wanted to play music, correction, *learn* how to play music. I didn't really care if we 'made it' or not, which pissed a few people off."

"Did you play any shows?"

"In our minds, yes. Dozens."

He laughs.

"In the real world? None that I can remember."

"I have to admit that I do care about making it."

"To each his own," I say. "As long as people aren't psycho about it, I don't care. I just love music too much to suck at it publicly."

"Well, I think we should see this show at the Coconut Teazer this weekend. What do you think? Are you into it?"

"I think I could be free."

"Why don't you meet me there on Saturday night around 9:30, and we'll check it out."

We make our goodbyes and hang up. Is it me, or does this not sound like a date now? He doesn't have to pick me up—he lives much closer to the venue than I do—but meet me there? Is that a little strange or what? I can't say Freddie didn't warn me.

The Coconut Teazer is a bright purple rock club on the corner of Sunset Blvd. and Crescent Heights. Thankfully, it's got a parking lot, accessible for a few extra bucks, because I would have no idea where to leave my precious but aging Volkswagen around here. Bob is hanging out, in a clean t-shirt and ratty jeans with a gas station attendant jacket.

"Hey," he says, grabbing me in a bear hug.

"Hey yourself."

"Let's go in. I already got us some tickets."

OK, so he paid, which kind of seems like a date. I don't feel so stupid for wearing the nicest dress I own, a light blue vintage number with rhinestone clips at the neckline. As I follow Bob through the throng of people toward the front, I catch a few guys looking at me, but I don't know how to handle the attention. I wish I could be "that girl," who knew what to do with all this.

Bob yells over the din, "You want a beer? I'm going to get one."

"Sure," I yell back, and duck my head to get some money out of my jacket.

"Don't worry about it. You can get the next round."

He comes back with beers in giant trophy glasses, almost like chalices. I try to drink daintily from it, but it's all over when the beer comes spilling over the lip and onto my dress.

"Oopsie," he says. I have never heard a guy use that term before. Truth be told, I've never heard anyone older than, say, ten use it either.

I wipe it away with my fingertips, and discretely onto the hem of my jacket. People around us begin to applaud as the band takes the stage. Well, platform is more like it. The stage area is marginally higher than the floor where we're standing, and it's hard to see the band over the taller people in front of us. But once the music starts, Bob is into it, moving his body aggressively in time with the drums and smacking his knee into the side of my leg every once in awhile. I try not to wince too much, and instead just move a step or two away. He doesn't seem to notice.

A few songs in, I yell to him that I'm going to get another beer, but his head is down. Finally, I give up, and just move to the bar. I feel eyes on me as I walk, and someone in my wake. When I get to the bar, I scream to the guy back there, barely discernible for the tattoos and poor lighting. I wonder if there are any spare places on his skin left undecorated.

Someone taps me on the shoulder, and I whip around, nearly whapping him with my hair. It's a guy, around my age, from the looks of it, though I'm terrible at figuring that kind of stuff out.

"Can I get those for you?" he asks, his brown eyes soft behind the glitter and eyeliner. He's reaching for his wallet, which makes me laugh. Chivalry from a rock dude.

"No, that's all right," I say, hoisting two glasses and trying not to smash into anyone. Luckily, the band seems to have magnetized most of the crowd to that side of the floor.

He follows me a few steps, keeping pace on my right flank. "What's your name?"

"Alyson," I shout.

"I'm Jim."

"As in Morrison?"

"As in Osterberg."

I smile, and he knows I get it, and I'm actually having a better time in these two minutes than I will have with Bob all night. But I don't know that yet.

"Nice," I say, grinning and disappearing into the crowd again. Bob is still rocking out, though thankfully not throwing devil horns or anything that craven. I hold out a beer to him and he almost knocks it out of my hand, turning toward me.

"Where did you go?"

I hold up the beers, which I hope will suffice as an explanation. My, we're being awfully possessive, for someone who didn't even seem to notice me before I left. He nods, lowering his head to drink his down.

"You like them?" he yells.

"Yeah, they're all right." Truth is, I'm not feeling this at all. I can't figure out if this is a date, a friendly get together for fellow music fans, or if I've been suddenly been appropriated as a wing-lady. I'm getting this weird vibe.

I notice Bob's eyes move around the room between songs, and land on someone in particular. I turn around, half expecting to find some buxom rock chick, complete with White Snake hair and a pair of dangerous stilettos. I never could walk in those damn things. But it's just Jim, of the cute smile and soft brown eyes encircled with blackish starlight.

I look back at Bob, then to Jim again. Jim smiles at me; Bob doesn't.

Is he fucking gay?

I don't have much of a chance to figure it out. A few songs later, Bob says he's got to get up early and hugs me goodbye. One of those hugs where your bodies hardly touch at all, and you just want it to end as soon as possible.

Clearly, I need more practice, but it's all I seem to get these days. Shouldn't I be better at his by now? I watch Bob's back walking away and hope it doesn't get weird in the future, since he knows two of my best friends here. I half consider turning around and having sex with Jim in the bathroom, but I just feel washed out and alone, old before my time.

My head's killing the next afternoon, though I haven't had much to drink the night before. Three, four beers max. If taste is any measure, the beer was cheap as shit, though, which may be the reason. Staggering to the bathroom, I chew four aspirin and feel the contents of my stomach grumble in protest. I splash water on my face and try to dig out some dried mascara from my tear ducts, which has made my crying black.

A few slugs of diet soda, and I'm feeling my legs under me again. I should eat something more substantial than a few crackers, but I have to be at work in less than an hour, and am praying that the food truck is there to tide me over. Manuel, the guy who works there, makes me feel like there's hope in having a family some day. He has pictures of his little girl everywhere, to remind him of what he's working for. His eyes are kind and sometimes tired.

A few more slugs and another can for the road. I pull on a reasonably clean t-shirt and polyester skirt over black leggings. One of my boots is missing, so I'm forced to resort to the black lace-up shoes my friend Yael calls the "dead grandfather shoes," because he's convinced I bought them at a yard sale at his grandparent's house, before we knew each other. If so, his grandfather had little feet, but I like the shoes just the same. Classic and, most importantly, flat. I am feeling particularly tall today.

It's late afternoon when I arrive, and the shift before us is breaking up. Tonight, I'm working with Jemma, a new manager. She shakes my hand when we meet, and explains that I gave her one of the test readings before I was hired, but that our shifts have been different so far, so we've not had the chance to work together. I scan my memory banks for a few seconds before I realize *oh yes, the singer.*

Jemma is tall and pretty, with creamy light brown skin. When everyone leaves, we catch up since the last time we spoke.

"How's the singing coming along?"

She completely ignores me, holding her hands out to the side, about a foot off her body, moving them downward.

I turn back to my desk. "Sorry," she says, finally. "I have to envelop myself in white light before each shift. It helps to keep the vampires away."

I have no idea what that means, but I smile anyway. "I remember that you're a very creative person. You did more than one thing, though, right?"

"Yes, I have the singing, but I also act. My manager's arranging a one-woman show for me, which you saw, correctly, was coming up in October."

"I remember. How did it go?"

"Great so far. He's got a few theaters booked. So we'll have to see if it all comes together as you saw it."

There's a twinge of embarrassment as I remember buttering her up shamelessly, hungry for a job and lying about travel and success and money. Jemma praised my sensitivity, and passed me along to round two, reading Martin. But that's another story.

Patrice is there, too, though she's off at a desk in the corner, bent over a legal pad. I can't tell if she's drawing or writing, so I give her a little wave and leave her to it. There's a portable stepper near the coffee machine, so I ask if I can use it.

Jemma waves me over. "Knock yourself out. I don't use those, though."

I get on, starting to move my legs up and down. It's not bad, for a portable model. I could do this all night. "Why not?"

"Oh, I used to be a competitive bodybuilder, so I just like to do . . . more when I work out."

That *more* is just so tempting, but I've promised myself to try and get along with others, play nice in the sandbox and all. Just because I can see her weaknesses doesn't mean I have to push on them, right?

"Wow, what was that like?"

Out of the corner of my eye, I can see Patrice turn toward us, roll her eyes theatrically, and go back to her pad. Jemma's only too happy to tell me. "Well, I've always been interested in fitness, ever since I was a dancer as a child." With this, she flicks her eyes up and down my body competitively. But I'm not playing.

"Then I had to keep my instrument fine tuned and ready. A singer and actress never knows when she'll need to travel, or learn a new skill. And then there's the weight issue." Again, she looks me up and down, and I wonder if we're really all that different in size. She's taller and more muscular, and maybe I'm heavier by a few pounds. Who freakin' cares?

My legs keep moving, up and down, up and down, and the rhythm of it lulls me into a daydream state. I watch her mouth, which never stops moving, but I'm only catching parts of it.

". . . always eat one almond a day because it keeps cancer away . . . lifted three times my body weight . . . three major prizes and a belt . . . drink lemon water with cayenne six times a day . . . met him one day while I was training . . ."

I step and nod, step and nod, and keep that stupid smile on my face. My gaze drifts over to Patrice, who's smiling at me, the phone to her ear on a call. She shakes her head as if to say *you asked for it, idiot. Now we've both got to deal with her.*

It's a slow night, and about an hour later, we hear a mighty slam against the south wall of our office. The three of us jump simultaneously, then Jemma is up out of her seat to investigate. I imagine her wielding a shield and a sword, like some sort of marauding Amazon with something to prove. She could probably lift anyone she might find, spin them around several times over her head, and deposit them back where she found them. The dizzying strategy. You can look it up.

"What the eff?" I whisper to Patrice. But she's unimpressed.

"That's the sex line. They're always getting into fights over there."

"Physical fights? Like punching fights?'

"Yeah, unfortunately." Patrice seems bored with the whole thing, while I feel oddly and ashamedly titillated.

Jemma comes back a few minutes later. I can hear her breathing coming a little faster. "I told them to keep it down, that we're trying to provide spiritual support for our callers. Idiots."

She returns to her chair, eyes blazing. "I have no idea why they even have a sex line next door to a psychic line."

A thought crosses my mind. "Are they owned by the same company?"

Jemma nods. She comes out from behind the desk again, holding out her hands to us. "Let's do a little purification ritual," she says. "I feel disgusting from their energy."

Dutifully, we take her hands, though I can tell that Patrice would rather eat ground glass, and I just want to go next door and stare in at the sex phone operators like zoo animals.

"Good, now let's visualize a cocoon of white light all around each one of us, and then joining us all together. We're stronger in a group than one by one."

I close my eyes and try to visualize some white light around us, but it has the consistency of a white light condom, kind of stretchy. When I let it go with my imagination, it snaps back on us, and I can almost feel the others recoiling from the blow.

A few minutes later, Jemma calls it off and returns to her seat. I go back to my books, Patrice returns to her drawing, and Jemma pulls out a dress she's sewing from a brown paper bag and begins to work on it in earnest. That's one skill I definitely don't have.

An hour or so later, Jemma goes out for a break. What she does out there I don't know, since she doesn't appear to eat, drink or smoke. Maybe she lifts the building off its foundation a few times and runs around the block.

When she's safely out of hearing range, Patrice leans over to me. "Did you ever hear such a load of bullshit? She's the worst one here, pretending she's going to be an actress. Please."

"You know, I don't care, as long as she doesn't fuck with me."

But Patrice is unmoved. "She's ridiculous. I hate working with her."

Jemma comes back just then, wearing the wrinkled face of concern. "I saw that car again, the black one? You know the one I mean?"

We look at each other, then back to Jemma. "I haven't," I say, and Patrice just keeps her eyes on Jemma, without comment. "What car?"

"There's this black car that kind of looks like a limousine, and it's always outside at night, if you have those shifts. It's always driving back and forth, back and forth."

That's starting to creep me out.

"Are they lost?" I ask.

"Maybe once, but they're always there."

"You're sure it's the same car."

Patrice pipes up, unable to keep quiet any more, "Wait, let me guess, it's the government."

Jemma gives her a disdainful look. "Well, the government does have a program for psychics and remote viewers. They have the ability to monitor any phone line they want, and they're always looking for new recruits."

"How do you know this?" Patrice doesn't even bother to hide her revulsion.

She looks at Patrice sweetly, but with a hint of malice underneath. "Some of us have access to all kinds of information, Patrice. That's why we work here."

What have I gotten myself into now?

"So you think we're all being recruited to be psychic spies for the government?"

"Stranger things have happened, Patrice. Remember—karma, karma."

I don't think either of us have any idea what she's talking about, but for the rest of the night, I can't get it out of my head, that every move we make is being watched, every person we talk to is being recorded, and every energy we accurately pick up is placing us one step closer to Uncle Sam's doorstep. I don't sleep well that night, or the next.

A few days later, Christmas cards begin to arrive, though I've been too busy at work to remember a major holiday like that one coming up. Birthday cards, too, for my Sag beginnings. The books say we love freedom, and that's very true. I can't stand people telling me how to think or what to do. We're alleged to be seekers, check, outdoorsy, yup, and sometimes insensitive. I try not to be, but sometimes the truth slips out. I seem to have been absent the day the mute buttons, or what I call the "dumb down buttons," were handed out.

I hang my cards on a string in the kitchen, and buy two strands of white lights at a local drug store. It looks a little more festive, but I still can't get over the 85-degree temperatures and the palms trees swaying lazily outside my window. Maybe I should find Santa somewhere, have a talk with him. There's a pang of very deep longing for the sharp winds of December in New York and just as quickly, it's gone. I have a new life, and this is it, like it or not.

There is news in the cards, of friends gossiping back and forth about my breakup, over a year now since it's happened. There are false reports of my incipient craziness, and ridiculous rumors about how I've been depressed, lonely and suicidal in Los Angeles, and will be coming home soon in defeat. I'm losing friends without even trying. But even if I wanted to go back, which I don't, I can feel that door, heavy as reinforced steel, clanging shut behind me.

I am here now, for the duration. I can feel it.

Taking out my cards, I shuffle them on the floor. Now they feel warm and familiar in my hands, like an extension of me. There are no more romanticized visions in my head, of being powerful or magical. I don't believe I can do any more of any less than someone else with my ability. I can do this thing, at this point in time, and I hope it can help people. That's all.

The Lovers comes up, and the Three of Cups. I feel about as celebratory as a Joy Division song, but when the cards talk, I have learned to listen. The Four of Wands and then a King, of Swords. Good with his hands, with his words. A take-no-prisoners kind of man.

As a writer, I'm thrilled by the prospect of a fellow wordsmith. Maybe he writes songs, or poems, or articles for the newspaper. But almost immediately, doubt sets in.

Though I'm supposed to be the expert here, dispensing romantic wisdom all day long, I wonder, like them, how I'll know the right one when I see him.

Are we like lighthouses in the night, sending out our energy like a beacon to our intended? Is there really destiny, where two people are magnetized for life? Or are we just renters of each other's time and company, waiting for the next tenant to show up?

Can two people ever really be meant for one other? And how, pray tell, can you know?

An answer, of sorts, shows up the next day. I wish I could say it was a hot guy, a Fedex deliveryman or something like that, and that our eyes locked over the chiles relleno at the taco truck. But that's not what happened.

It's a call I get, about halfway through my shift. From the sound of his voice, he's a teenager, though he says he's twenty-three. He drawls his words in a thick Southern accent that's almost comical. But I'm not here to judge.

"I'm worried about my sex life," he says.

"All right. Do you want me to see if there's a new partner coming in for you?" Since you never know who they're into, you learn to use the gender-neutral terms.

"There's no more girls in Tennessee. I seen 'em all by now I reckon."

"Let me take a look." I shuffle and spread the cards into a cross. "Well, I can see a lot of girls around you. Lots of them."

"That's good," he laughs.

"Really, I'm not kidding. There are several girls for you to pick from. Why don't you ask one of them out?" I don't know why, but I'm feeling protective of this kid.

"Well, there's this little problem. I don't last in bed."

"Are you sure you don't want to talk to someone on the sex line, Tom? I'm a psychic, so I can't help you there."

"No, I want to talk to you. I have to deal with this problem."

"It's a pretty common issue. Maybe if you're having sex with a woman, you'll get comfortable with her, and it won't be a problem anymore."

"See, the problem is, I play with myself constantly."

Deep water, getting deeper. But I refuse to let a kid think that playing with himself is dirty.

"Lots of people do that. Don't worry about it. When you're having more sex, you probably won't want to masturbate so much anymore."

I look around, and Katie is staring at me, making faces and trying to get me to laugh. *Bitch.* She makes masturbating motions with her right hand, mimes a blowjob, the whole thing.

"Yeah, but even when I have sex a few times a day, I still want to play with myself all the time. It makes me ashamed and worried."

"Have you ever heard of tantric sex? Maybe you could try that, and learn how to control your body a little more, so you can have more pleasure."

"No, ma'am."

"Maybe you could get a book about it, or look at medical books about women's bodies. When you understand how they work, maybe it will subside."

"Well, I've tried some of that. Not the tantric stuff, but the pictures of women's bodies. But all I can ever think about is masturbating."

I lay down a few more cards. He's not lying to me.

"There's really nothing wrong with masturbation, as long as it's not done publicly."

"Well, that's the thing . . ."

I wait for the other shoe to drop, right on top of my head.

"Uh huh?"

"What I really like to go is go into the K-Mart dressing room and masturbate there."

I have to cover a laugh, with Katie making ridiculous sexual gestures and the mental image of him, under the harsh green light in the big box store.

When I recover, I say, "Well, that's probably not good. Maybe you need to see a therapist, who could help you sort out these problems."

"But I want to know why I have it. Can you ask the cards about that?" It's such a desperate plea that I gather up the cards I've laid out and spend a few more seconds laying out another spread.

"I can see that you have trouble relating to woman, that's why you'd prefer to get yourself off without them."

"All right, then. Well, I have to go to the bathroom, and you know . . ." The phone bangs in my ear, and I'm left with another image I'll spend all night trying to erase.

The answer, as I see it, to all my lofty questions about connection? It's happening all around you, babe, from the low to the high and back again. You think you have special needs that everyone in the world doesn't have? You think you're different?

Let me tell you one perfect thing. You're exactly like everyone else.

The year ends with a party of sorts, with Opal, her ex-husband Nigel and her new boyfriend, along with her roommate and a few others I don't know. She's three drinks in and raring to go when I arrive, and it takes Nigel all of seven minutes to start paying footsie with me under the table. We've been doing thus for a little over a month now, making prolonged eye contact, adjusting each other's clothing or letting an innocent touch linger. He's tall and blond with bright blue eyes like marbles and a sexy Scottish accent. Normally, I can't understand a word, but with him I know all I need to know.

Kyle, Opal's new boyfriend, is in the kitchen boiling a bunch of Chinese herbs (sticks and bark, mostly), into a foul smelling liquid that's thick as molasses. He's got a cold, and isn't planning on missing out on New Year's just because his body won't cooperate. I make the mistake of sneezing, due probably to Opal's cat, and he's pouring me a shot of this viscous shit like it's Macallan's and urging me to drink it.

"You have asthma, right?"

I nod, doubtfully. How I'm going to get it down my throat I have no idea.

"You gotta try this. The Chinese doctor said it opens the lungs and clears everything out."

I look over at Kyle and he's smiling, just waiting to see what I'll do. I take the glass in one hand and a beer in the other, and down the herbs in one go. The beer follows, chasing the acrid taste of foliage from my palate.

Then we're in someone's car and he's driving fast across Wilshire, up La Cienega and then I can't even see where we are. Nigel's hand is on my leg and I'm feeling warm and rubbery from the beer, and wired up inside, like I could dance all night. We stop at Dragonfly, on Santa Monica, and the music is so loud we can't hear each other. I follow Opal's pink and blue scarves as they wind behind her in the crowd. Nigel's hand is on my back and then my ass, and we're undulating like a huge viper making our way to the back porch area. Someone gets us all drinks, then another, and I'm slow dancing with Nigel, face pressed into his smooth chest left open by his collar.

He whispers that maybe we can go out to the beach later and watch the sunrise, and I can't think of a better way to mark the new year.

But the Chinese herbs are churning in my stomach and I'm off to the dance floor, where the bodies are bouncing and wheeling, arms in, arms out, the multi-colored lights like candy on everyone's faces. I'm dancing with no one, I'm dancing with everyone, and then I'm dancing with Quentin Tarantino. Really. He moves in close, grooving along to the music, making eye contact.

"Hey," he says, with that cool thing going on. "What's your name?"

"Alyson." I should be out of breath, but amazingly, I'm not. This shit is incredible.

"I'm Quentin. I make movies."

This seems so hilarious to me that I collapse into his chest, giggling. He holds me there for a few minutes, then takes my hands and spins me around. I never want this feeling to end, this anarchic, childlike bopping around. We dance for a few more minutes, until Nigel wades into the fray. Quentin, my brush with fame, fades into the melee, and we don't talk again.

There's more drinking when I get back outside—a few bottles of champagne lined up, with cheap plastic glasses designed to look expensive. I'm not ready to toast, though. I just feel electric and don't want to stop moving. I'm like one of those fish that dies when it sits still for too long.

I've got my arms around Nigel's neck and it seems like everything is groovy when he says he can't give me a ride home. I'm far too drunk to drive, and don't understand. But Opal explains that he has to fix her cabinet tomorrow.

I've never been totally sure about their relationship, but it starts to dawn on me that something weird's going on. Nigel seems mortified that he's told me one thing and now has to do another.

"That's fine. You can sleep on my couch." Opal says brightly. "It'll be like a girly sleepover party!"

That's the last thing on my mind, and I feel like crying for a few seconds. But then everyone is toasting and honking into little plastic horns and kissing each other. Nigel kisses me, long and sweet, on the lips, then whispers, "Sorry" into my ear.

The herbs are finally wearing off, and I feel exhausted by all the dancing, all the flitting about, all the flirting. I'm just a relatively young woman, inebriated and hungry, looking for some sort of connection in the wide world. Then I want to be home, in my own bed, warm under the covers to start fresh. But we're off, dragging ourselves back to the car and Beverly Hills before the sun comes up.

January

☆ Capricorn ☆

I am coming back down to earth.

"Hi, are you the psychic?"

"Yes, I just need to get a few pieces of information from you before we start. What's your name?"

"Jerry."

"And what's your date of birth, please?"

"The 26ᵗʰ of June, 1972."

His voice sounds familiar, but my head is so fuzzy, I can't place it right now.

"All right, then. How can I help you?'

"Well, there's this woman, and she keeps leaving messages on my answering machine going 'stop it, stop it, stop it' and I'm not sure if it's my ex-girlfriend or not. Can you see if it's her?"

Ah, yes. John, Joe, Jim, Jerry. I shuffle the cards and lay them out across my desk.

"I can see that you've had a bad breakup with someone recently, and are looking for a way to stay connected."

"Stay connected? That bitch caused me so much trouble, I couldn't be happier that she's out of my life. I just want to know if she's leaving me these messages or not."

I can feel a headache starting to pound behind my eyes. A few more cards go down.

"To tell you the truth, Jerry, I don't see that she is leaving the messages. Maybe it's one of her friends, or just someone with a wrong number. But the sooner you can let her go, the better for both of you."

"But she's harassing me with these phone calls! She can't do that!"

"If you think it's a matter for the police, by all means, given them a call. But I don't see that she's the perpetrator."

Silence. It's the first time I've gotten him to shut up in five months of trying.

I'm so stunned that it's a few second before I can say, "Is there anything else I can help you with today?"

"No, that's it. Thanks." He's being sarcastic, but I don't care. Five more minutes on my timesheet, fifty more cents for my prodigiously bulging pocketbook. I pencil it in and promptly forget about it.

Katie is talking to a distraught young woman in one corner of the room. She's extremely large, with rippling, doughy flesh and eyes that sink back into her head like buttons. All I can see is pink—in her clothing, her purse and even her skin, which gives off a freshly scrubbed glow. She's sobbing, while Katie tries to comfort her.

Mercy's out smoking and Aaron's giving a horary reading on the phone. I go over to Katie and her friend.

"Hey," I say. "Are you all right?"

Katie is looking at me kind of pleadingly, though I don't know why. The woman looks up at me like a child.

"They said they would leave it. They told us again and again."

"Leave what?"

"They said they would leave us two bags of money, on our doorstep, so we could guard the Underground City of Telos."

I make eye contact with Katie, who shrugs, out of the woman's eye line.

"I don't know if you've met Alyson. She's kind of new around here. Alyson, this is Ciara."

"Hey." I stick out my hand and she takes it, but her energy feels like a damp rag and her hand has all the vitality of a dead snake.

"So they said you had to guard this underground city?"

"Yeah, the Underground City of Telos. It's under Mt. Shasta, and has been part of the Hollow Earth for centuries." She acts kind of annoyed, like I'm completely out of it for asking.

"It's Lemurian," Katie adds, making a face behind Ciara's back.

"Oh." Of course, I have no idea what they're talking about. If I remember correctly, Lemurian is one of those words associated with lost cities like Atlantis, but I can't be sure.

Ciara begins to cry again, this time more forcefully. "All I want to do is live in love consciousness. All I want to do is get rid of violence and negativity." She starts rocking back and forth, sobbing harder now.

"Maybe they're just late." Katie gives me a death look.

"No, they said they would put two paper shopping bags with money at our front door this morning. That's what they said."

"On the Ouija board," Katie says for my benefit.

"God, I'm terribly sorry," I say, confused and too open to her pain right now. I want to go back to my desk and rewind time, so I don't have to hear this crazy story. "But maybe they'll come another time."

Ciara puts her head down on her chest, crying and shaking her head no. She knows it won't happen, but the crushing disappointment won't let go.

I go back to my desk and try to read, but I can't get the image of the child-woman trapped in all that flesh out of my mind. All of us are searching for something, but with our gifts, shouldn't we be able to see it a little better?

An hour or so later, Martin comes in and stands in the doorway. He whisks my phone sheet off my desk and says, "Come with me, please."

I look around for support, but Mercy's head is down, pretending to read. Katie just looks at me, then to Mercy.

I follow Martin upstairs, thinking about the solar eclipse happening today.

"Come in," he commands, and I do. He slams the door behind me as I sit down.

He refuses to look at me, but instead types relentlessly into the computer. His normally tanned face is white with anger.

I wait for him to begin. After a full ten seconds of silence, Martin asks, "What's your problem?"

"I don't know what you're talking about."

"Everyone's telling me you have an attitude problem."

"I'm not sure I understand what you mean." I wonder who comprises "everyone."

"Look at this sheet from yesterday and tell me why you don't want to work here anymore."

Dutifully, I take the sheet and scan it. Not like I've forgotten yesterday's motley lineup that fast. The hold times are average, maybe a little low.

I wonder which of the managers has narc'd. But it doesn't take long for the finger to point to Mercy, the one who'd sell her grandmother's foundation garments for ten minutes alone with Martin.

"Can't get it?" he asks.

I shake my head. Then, an idea comes. "You mean my problem with the lottery numbers?"

He goes rigid, no doubt thinking of the money I could've made him. I imagine the numbers flooding through his brain, impregnating it with tiny coinlike children.

"That's what you're angry about?"

"I'm not angry." The sexual tension is coming off him in waves.

I take a deep breath. "Okay. It was a very slow day, and the energy in the room was really weird. The sex line people got into another fist-fight next door, so two calls hung up on me because they couldn't hear anything but screaming. That, and you were yelling at Mercy, and so three more ended the calls earlier than they would have."

I stop there, unwilling to tell on the rest of the readers, who routinely combine the times of several calls to make it look like one long one.

"You're always complaining," Martin asserts, still trying lamely to manufacture his argument.

"I have no idea what you're talking about. I don't create scheduling problems, I'm always on time, and if having a bad attitude means I come to work, I do my job, then I go home and don't get involved in the politics of this place, then yes, I do have a bad attitude."

I sit back in my chair and flatten my hands along the padded arms. I try to quiet my raging mind, forcing my fingers to remain still.

"Why are you so calm?" Martin asks, eyeing the corners of the room for moral support.

"I have nothing to lose."

His face cracks open, all warmth and good will. "Can we work this thing out with the lottery numbers if I promise to get the managers to keep the noise level down while you're reading?"

"I guess so. I don't like it, though, and I'll do this under protest. I'd prefer to transfer the calls unless there's no one else to take them."

"Deal." Martin rises and shakes my hand.

The room downstairs is silent when I come back in. Katie is sitting with her back to Mercy, who's throwing down cards and biting her nails with a vengeance.

Katie looks up between her lashes. "Do you still work here?"

"Yeah."

I go back to my desk, my back pointedly faced toward the manager who's failed to defend me. My friend, who's fed me to the dogs.

I turn to Katie. "I don't think I'll be doing any more socializing at this job. Sorry, but having a personality seems to be strictly forbidden." I settle into a book.

Mercy looks stricken with conscience. Behind my hand, I wink at Katie. Silently, we agree to a good head fucking.

I vow to quit as soon as I can. I have skills; I have talent. I don't need this shit.

The next morning, I take my place at my desk in a woolly blanket of silence. Mercy can barely meet my gaze as I punch in, so I turn my back and read Susan Faludi, hating that women routinely betray each other for men.

For an hour, not a word is spoken. I drink a Diet Coke, put my feet on my desk and read. When a call comes in, I do a reading. But no more.

Mercy chain-smokes and plays computer solitaire. It's about as close to real risk-taking as she'll likely get in this lifetime. I can see from here that her nails are bitten to the quick.

Katie arrives a little later and we exchange wry smiles, planning our subterranean revenge. At nine-thirty, we go to the food truck together, a small act of rebellion in itself, since there are no readers to take the calls but Mercy herself.

The truck is our one connection with outside reality, stranded as they are in the industrial outskirts of Playa del Rey.

"We could quit together, or we could make it miserable for everyone." That's why I like Katie in the first place. She's full of venom and strategy.

I counter, "Maybe we could sabotage Martin's astrology class."

"Maybe . . ." But Katie's mind is working in far eviler directions.

I complete her sentence. "The best way would be to sleep with Martin. That would kill her."

Katie dissolves into burbling laughter, doubling over and supporting herself with a palm against the side of the truck. "But you'd have to touch him."

We pay for the soda and breakfast burritos, our standard fare, and exchange a last joke with the driver. When Martin comes in later that day, he squeezes my shoulder on his way by my desk. "Good morning, dear," he sings.

I try not to flinch as his hand contacts my flesh. Weakly, I respond, "Hello there."

When Mercy meets my gaze, her eyes are cold and filled with hatred. Love, however deluded, does these things to people.

On the way home, I stop by the nearest Staples and corner the market on printer ink, fancy resume paper and mailing labels. By the time I've paid for everything, I wonder how I'm going to afford stamps, no less groceries. But I don't care. I need to get out of this terrible job, and start making real money, so I can finally be an adult.

Driving home, I begin to picture what a real, adult life would look like. Maybe I'd own a vacuum cleaner, instead of having to drive to West Hollywood to borrow one from a friend every time I want to clean my apartment. Maybe I'd own clothing that cost more than $2-3 bucks per piece, or hadn't been worn by at least one other person before me. Maybe, if I were really lucky, I'd have a mate (the mind unfortunately goes blank here, unable to picture it in real life) who was supportive and loving and not a bum or a junkie or a weirdo. Or maybe a weirdo, but in a good way.

I'm so used to doing everything alone that I can't imagine someone chipping in for the phone bill, or helping me clean up before company comes over or holding my hand when I'm sad about a reading I've had that day. The weight of this loneliness hits me square in the chest and the tears are flowing under my sunglasses before I can stop them. I didn't have enough money to buy tissues *and* resume paper, so I wipe my sadness away with the collar of my t-shirt, smearing makeup into it. Maybe, if I give this shirt away one day, someone else will wear my sadness around, someone poor as me, down on their luck and looking for the realest kind of love there is.

At home, I push through the want ads and the printing out of cover letters and the envelope stuffing and minor blessing over each one before it goes in a pile by the door to be mailed. Still weeping a bit, I drink three beers before I realize I've done it, and am feeling very tipsy when I stand up. I look at the phone, imagining the drunken camaraderie, if not the fuck 'em all conversation courtesy of my New York friends. It's late there, but maybe they're up for a semi-tearful call from their long-lost California babe. Not like it hasn't happened before . . .

I pick up the phone and start dialing. On the third try, I get someone.

"Hey you," he says. "What's goin' on in sunny Cali?"

"I just needed to talk to someone." I know I sound small.

He drags deep from a cigarette and I am shocked by how close his breath sounds as he exhales. "Well, you've come to the right place. I can't sleep. Tell me what's going on, baby."

The resumes have been mailed; the prayers have been said. If I knew a rain dance or a cosmic chant, I would do them as well, naked if necessary. I honor and respect all spiritual deities and ask all of them to bond together like a mighty Justice League of Get Alyson a New Fucking Job, combining their awesome talents and weaponry to do this one thing. I promise anyone listening that I will pay it back, or extend the same to others if I could just get the hell out of that room and its needy people struggling to feel love, just like me.

Maybe it's the mirror aspect of the whole endeavor, or just the sinking reality of not being able to afford food and rent in the same week. Something's gotta give, and it's probably going to be groceries. Maybe there's a food bank nearby. Calls home result in nothing more than tales of their own financial stress, or worries that they may not have enough in the future, hence their inability to lend me some money now.

I want to stop thinking about this, so I pool my change and drive to Vidiots to rent something happy. Not quite in the mood for a romantic comedy, but something funny and hopeful and ultimately capable of blasting me out of my head and into someone else's.

I go to bed the night of January 16th tired. Though I haven't heard back from any of my mailed resumes, I have been on a writing tear, working on a new screenplay. I don't even know if it's something anyone would buy, or something I might want to make myself, and I don't care. It just feels good to let that part of me sing again, free and unfettered.

My fingers are flying over the keys until my eyes start to become heavy. I push past it once and then twice before my mind just won't cooperate anymore. I forget the name of the character I'm writing about, backspace and type it over three times wrong before I save the document and call it a night. Washing my face, I wish it were tomorrow, so I could get to work on it again.

I have an early shift tomorrow, with Radar, so I try to empty my mind and fall asleep as soon as I can. The early morning callers are notorious for their desperation, as if they've been up all night, wrestling with their demons.

I've been asleep for maybe twenty minutes when the ground begins to rumble like a hundred pissed-off monster trucks harnessed together. The first jolt is so violent and loud, I hit the floor on my shoulder and roll to the wall, bumping my nose. I have no idea what to do, so I try to stagger to my feet, but our building is set in sand, and seems to be waving back and forth in the wind. Three stories of brick isn't enough to protect any of us. I stagger around like a drunk, the ground shifting beneath my feet. Are you supposed to stand in a doorframe, or go under a table during an earthquake? I don't have a table, so I try to crawl to the doorframe between my bedroom and the hallway.

I can hear my neighbor outside, slamming his door. "Alyson? You all right in there?"

"Yeah," I yell. "I'm OK." I'm clutching onto the doorframe so hard my fingers are white. Finally, the shaking stops, but I can't seem to let go.

"We're going downstairs to see if the building's all right."

In the next few moments, a cacophony of human voices roused from sleep sounds. Some are shouting and others are opening and shutting their doors, running down the stairs with heavy shoes. I sit on the floor in shock, breathing like I've just run a marathon.

Twenty seconds has felt like a thousand times that amount. I've heard the term *aftershock* before, but don't really know what that means. Now I can hear everyone outside, babbling and frightened, holding each other, some of them crying. I don't trust my legs yet, so I crawl over to the window and peer out. The streetlights illuminate a pieta of sorts. I recognize my neighbor across the hall and Kevin from downstairs, looking dazed. I wonder if he was high when the earthquake came. What an earthquake would be like while stoned, I don't want to find out.

For a few minutes, I sit on the rough carpeting in the dark, feeling the cold breeze on my neck and listening to the voices outside. The building seems to be in no danger of collapsing, but

I can hear sirens in the distance, their sounds already spiking the morning.

When it seems like we're safe, I get to my feet, feeling wobbly and uncertain. The floor is there to support my weight. I dress quickly in the dark, hearing my neighbors returning to their apartments. Somewhere I've read that earthquakes often produce lots of broken glass, so I want to make sure I have my boots on. Who knows if we'll be asked to evacuate?

It's around 5:00 now, and my shift starts at 6:00. We haven't had any aftershocks, whatever that means, but I'm not sure if I need to go to work or not. I call AstralPlanet, but the phone rings and rings, with no answer. I try all the switches and lights, and they're dead, too. No TV, and the only radio I have is on my boom box, with its decidedly dead batteries.

So I go to the sink and start doing the dishes. Maybe it'll be cleared up in a few minutes and I can get to my shift. A few minutes later, the phone rings, startling me. Outside, the sky is starting to lighten.

"Oh my God, are you OK?" It's my brother in Boston, his voice betraying his fear. "I was calling and calling, and couldn't get through."

"Sure," I say. "Why?"

"I'm looking at the footage from the earthquake on TV and it's unbelievable. Are you sure you're OK? You sound weird."

"Sure, yeah. I'm just doing the dishes. I have to be at work in a little while and I was afraid I would oversleep if I went back to bed."

"Dude, this looks really bad. I'm betting you don't have to go in to work."

"I don't know. If I don't go in, I don't get paid, you know?"

Even though he's younger, he tries to sound fatherly, a thing I'll come to appreciate with time. "Alyson, I really think you should stay home now until you know it's safe. I'm looking at whole sections of the freeway that have collapsed, and fires burning out of control. It's a lot worse than you may realize right now."

"Oh," I notice that my voice sounds really far away and wonder if I'm in shock. "Yeah, I don't have power, and I can't get the radio because my batteries are dead."

"Stay home for now, OK?"

"All right. Are you going to call Mom? I won't be able to get through to her."

"Yeah, don't worry about it. I'll call everyone. I just want you to promise me that you're not going anywhere."

"I'm not going anywhere."

He sounds relieved, as if he were dealing with an unruly child and has finally won the war. "Good. I'm calling you later, and I'm going to be mad if you're not there."

"I promise. The only reason I might go out is if I need food or water or batteries. That's it."

"OK." I can tell he doesn't want to hang up first.

"Thanks for calling, all right? I appreciate it."

"I'm just glad you're all right."

I try to get ahold of someone at Astral Planet for the next several hours, dialing, hearing that bleating *eh-eh-eh* of the circuits busy sound, hanging up. Finally, I'm so bored that all the dishes are done, the tile floor is swept and the bathroom sink is clean. All the clothes have been picked up from the floor, the dirty ones herded into a pile on the bed and the clean ones hung up in the closet. I've even sorted the books into piles: ones that have to go to the library, ones that can be sold back to the Bodhi Tree and ones I still have to read.

Throughout the morning, there have been sirens wailing and trucks of all kinds streaking up and down Pacific. I can hear more of them further out, and wonder if they're in Santa Monica, or West Hollywood, or Mar Vista. Where has the freeway collapsed? Are my friends all right?

I get a few more calls from my New York peeps and go through what I know, which is nothing, really. All of them have seen the footage on television, so even though they're there and I'm here, they know more than I do. All of them are glad to hear I'm alive and promise to send me supplies from New York. But all I want are slices of pizza, bialys smeared with melted butter, bagels with cream cheese and Indian food from 6th Street—things you can't mail, really.

The thought makes me hungry. My stomach has been growling for the past few hours, and the raisins and peanuts I've fed it haven't done much to quiet its demands. I have to admit that the curiosity is killing me. Even though I've promised my brother I wouldn't leave, I have to.

I'm going to. And taking my camera with me.

In the past, whenever I've seen films with heroic photojournalists, living together, crouching and sweating in some Latin American jungle or collapsing African dictatorship, some part of me identifies. Part of it is romantic, sure, but the other part is the pissed-off part of me, the righteously indignant bit that loves the Clash and wants justice at all costs. Maybe I think of myself a little like that in this moment, though I have no one to report to, no credentials or ticket out. My car might get me as far as Needles before it gave out.

The first thing I see, gratefully, is that my building is standing and intact. Walking all the way around it, I can see that we haven't sustained even a single crack. Maybe sand foundations are good for something. The second thing I see is a fallen house just two doors down. It's slid into the street like a base runner chugging for home. There's a massive gap in the blacktop at the corner of Main Street, like a zigzag of lightning. Already, I can see ants crawling out of the earth there, moving crumbs, sticks and bits of leaves below.

My camera hangs from my shoulder, unused. I just walk toward Santa Monica, stunned by the devastation. I understand why my brother sounded like he did when I see the broken appliances lying in the road, the glass smashed out of the storefronts and glittering on the sidewalk. Peering into one of the windows, I can see bookshelves that have been tossed about like children's toys, and once-desired merchandise crushed beneath. I snap a picture of this, and feel immediately guilty. I would make a terrible photojournalist.

The curious part of me is pulled along Main Street. I can see a house that has imploded under its own weight, with a dent in its roof and a sagging chimney. Every once in awhile, a car passes, but very few people are outside. In the distance, I can see two teenagers walking with skateboards in their hands, wide-eyed looks of wonder on their faces. Others dart to their cars with two-gallon jugs of water in each hand.

By the time I get to Santa Monica Boulevard, I'm far from home. But I don't care. I gaze one way, finding the placid sea, same as always. The other way is a different kind of sea, with waves of safety glass knocked from the car dealership windows. Sunlight dazzles off it like a mirage, and the cars are naked and exposed, completely stealable if anyone had a mind to do so.

But we're all so stunned that the glitter is on the ground now, not in the sky or the eyes of our idols, that we simply don't know how to act. At a liquor store, I buy some water, ramen and cookies, which should keep me alive until I don't know when. I've walked over five miles by the time I get home, and my legs are sore.

The phone service goes out for a few days, but when it comes back, I call Katie to see if she's gotten in touch with anyone from AstralPlanet. She answers on the first ring, sounding anxious. "Hello?"

"Hey it's me," I say.

"Oh my God, I thought you were my husband. He's been gone for over an hour, and he only went out to get milk."

"Do you know where he went?"

"I thought he went to Ralph's but now I'm not so sure. I might have to go out and look for him soon. What's going on?"

"Oh, I just wondered if you'd spoke with anyone from work. I can't seem to get through."

"Martin called me yesterday . . ."

I guess it pays to flirt.

". . . and said they had some problems with the lines from the earthquake."

"Oh, no one called me."

"They might have. I mean, we were supposed to have a phone tree, but you know how reliable everyone is at AstralfuckingPlanet."

"I do." It's good to hear her voice, which makes me feel a little more human. "But it's still weird that they didn't call me."

"They're supposed to let us know when the lines are back up and running. Maybe a few days at the most."

"Are you all right over there?"

"Yeah, the chimney's completely fucked, and there's a huge crack on the concrete by the pool. But other than that, we're doing pretty well."

"Good, I'm glad to hear it. Do you want to get off the phone in case Jermaine calls?"

"Yeah, dude. I'd better. But you keep on keepin' on, all right?"

It's hard to hide my disappointment. I want to be around people now, warm human bodies with actual human feelings. It'll make me feel less alien and afraid. "Well, if you want to get together do some channeling, I'm open," I say.

"OK, dude. I'll let you know."

For the next few days, I forget the callers. Every last one of them. I forget about John-Jerry-Joe and his weird whispered "stop it-stop it" phone calls, the K-Mart masturbator, the woman whose lover was killed in a car crash with four naked women. I forget the anguished voices of loneliness and the pleading if they don't get the answers they're seeking. But I realize that they comprise the bulk of human contact for me, since I haven't made that many friends in six months.

To pass the time, I reassure people back east. I throw readings for myself on the floor, trying to figure out if I'll have a job to go back to. I look as far into the future as the spirits will let me see, so I can determine if I have a future here at all. On the third day, I venture back to the Beverly Hills Library, encountering a freeway closure on the 10 East, which re-routes me through West L.A. and under the 405. Freeways have a sinister feeling to them now, and I hold my breath under overpasses, releasing it only when the light goes green.

The library is still closed, but I deposit my books into the return slot. Two trucks pass by, with people's belongings loaded into the beds, piled high and tilted precariously. They're heading east, to where I've come from just a few months ago. I wonder if I should follow them.

No matter what happens next, this is the end of one phase and the beginning of another.

After a few confusing days of near constant worry and hypothesizing phone conversations, I hear from Radar, who's been worried about me. It's odd to be standing in my living room talking to this near stranger who knows so much of my business. His voice sounds sincere, though, and I'm touched by his concern.

"You're the only other person at AstralPlanet who lives alone like me, so I wondered if you were all right."

"Well, it was definitely a shock."

"They don't have anything like that back in New York, do they?"

"Definitely not. I've seen a shooting, a riot, bar fights and all kinds of other stuff. I was even mugged once. But an earthquake I wasn't prepared for."

"Well, I have some good news, if you can call it that. The line was down for awhile, but they've been able to repair it and we're going to start up again next Monday. You're on the schedule from six to noon, and I figured you could get the rest of your schedule when you come in."

I scribble it down on a delivery menu. "Great, well, thanks for calling. It's really nice of you." Truth is, I don't want to hang up. It's the closest thing to companionship in days. This is someone from the trenches, someone who understands. This is a fellow Op, who sees more than meets the eye, like I do.

"All right, then. I'll see you on Monday."

We hang up, and I sit on the floor, looking at the cards spread out in front of me. I want more than anything to be among the other freaks, so I can feel as if I belong to something other than the cracked earth, our world balanced on the edge of a fault line.

New Yorkers don't have a corner on the gallows humor market, I realize with appreciation. Just when I've become convinced that everyone here has drunk deeply from the same Kool-Aid spring, I run into a guy with an I ♥ Plate Tectonics shirt in 7-11, where I've gone to get a Slurpee. There are very few of them in Los Angeles, at least in my area, and being in one reminds me of collecting baseball cups. My brother had so many that, stacked one inside the other, they reached almost as high as the ceiling. An image of him in Boston, a few months from becoming a father, fills my eyes with tears in the potato chip aisle.

I'm too shy to approach the Plate Tectonics guy, though he's pretty cute. Instead, I imagine that he's my boyfriend and that we do post-earthquake things together. Maybe we'd go out and buy enormous jugs of water, or choose canned meals that we'd share by flashlight. Maybe we'd snuggle closer at night, deprived of power or heat in the dead of winter, or knit blankets made from recycled concert t-shirts. Shit like that actually goes through my head.

At the register, I get ready to pay for stuff I can't really afford, standing right behind him. He pays for his stuff, which includes a selection of canned beef stew, rolling papers and two bottles of Mountain Dew. My kinda guy. He flashes me a smile before he leaves with his purchases, almost making my day. But in the next moment, I am alone again, and less certain than ever that this terrible time of crisis will pass.

Katie invites me over that weekend, where I meet her husband Jermaine, a cute English guy, her sister and brother-in-law. Somehow they make it work with two couples in one house, which has miraculously not sustained much damage in the earthquake. An arthritic white dog, a relic from Katie's childhood, meets me at the door with a baleful look before turning away with disinterest.

"Tica, will you fuck off?" The dog just looks at her before skulking away. "Hey," she says, giving me a hug. "Did you find it OK?"

"Yeah, just a lot of turns, that's all." My car is parked under a date palm shedding enormous leaves and I wonder if it's safe there. I guess we'll find out.

"I printed out a chart of the earthquake and wanted to show it to you." We make our way back to her room, which is stacked up with books on tarot, astrology, Buddhism and writing, all passions we share. Her desk is wedged into one corner, with an anemic lamp and papers blown every which way. A black cat winds itself around her ankles and she bends to pet it absently.

She hands me the printout, and I can see right away what happened. Uranus, planet of sudden and often violent change, is sitting right on the IC, the point at the very bottom of the chart, part of a tight stellium of planets in late Capricorn, including Venus and Neptune, along with Mercury in Aquarius.

Katie's biting her lip. "What do you think?"

"Wow, I can't believe all that energy at the bottom of the chart."

"I know . . ."

"Uranus?" I say, laughing. "Literally, it's shaking the ground up."

"What about the other stuff, though?"

"Oh my God, look at this. It's all conjuncting the natal Pluto in the 4th, opposing Mercury in the 10th, and squaring the nodes."

"What the hell are you seeing, Math Geek?"

"I don't know. It just looks so intentional."

"You mean karmic?"

"Yeah, karmic, but also that it was supposed to be in our lives, for some reason."

"Why, so we can get FEMA money?" She's laughing, but her eyes are lined, I notice, from lack of sleep. Everyone's been a bit touchy since that night.

"No, not that. It just feels like we were supposed to be here, for some reason."

For the next few hours, we obsess, the way most psychics do, putting most detectives to shame with our capacity to go over covered ground. We run composites with our natal charts and the earthquake, the earthquake and our relocation charts (neither of us is from L.A. originally), and even a composite with AstralPlanet and the earthquake, hoping these documents will give us some perspective on what will come.

My own charts emphasize two aspects. In my relocation chart it's the 1st house, of self-expression and how I project myself into the world, that's packed with planets. The 10th has a few surprises as well, with Jupiter on the MC and Pluto conjuncting the North Node. In my natal composite, several planets populate the 10th as well, with Mercury, the Sun, the Moon and Jupiter in close proximity.

Traditionally, the 10th is the father or father figure, the career and one's own authority. But I have none of those. I've been estranged from my father for years, and have no career to speak of. Though I left behind lucrative gigs writing and editing in New York, there is none of that going on here. And being a psychic doesn't seem to come with much of a retirement plan.

"I can't figure out how the earthquake is going to change my career," I say, handing my chart to Katie for inspection.

She looks it over, furrowing with concentration. "Maybe you'll get a great writing job soon."

"Or maybe I'll be homeless."

"Maybe you'll write about this someday."

"I doubt it," I say, grabbing the chart back from her. "Do you have any beer?"

Work commences on Monday the 24th, a week after the earthquake. Though normally I'm grumbling my ass off about getting up early for my 6:00 AM shift, I'm acting like one of those Disney dwarves, whistling to myself as I brush my teeth and exchanging inane pleasantries with the guy in the gas station as I nab my dual Diet Dr. Peppers.

Radar is there, his nose in a book, when I arrive. I can see that he's been making stuff. His scissors and scraps of cloth lay nearby.

"Alyson!" he says when I walk in. It's as effusive as I've ever seen him, shy as he is, and I immediately walk over to him and give him a big hug. There's nothing weird or awkward or sexual about it. "I've been making these for everyone, but this one is for you." He hands me a beautiful handmade medicine bag, strung on a leather cord, with a stitched design on the front and a lump inside I can feel with my thumb.

"It's so lovely. Thank you," I say, overcome with all kinds of feelings. I'm a complete jerk for not getting him, or anyone, anything for the holidays.

"I put a sodalite in there for you. It's supposed to give you inner peace, and is good for writers."

"That's the best, thanks," I say, putting it around my neck and not even caring that it doesn't go with what I'm wearing. I feel protected and strong all day.

"I'm sorry I didn't get you anything."

He smiles, looking at his shoes. "That's not necessary. I just wanted to give you that."

Maybe it's possible for people to not suck.

Or maybe not. An hour into my first shift back, a woman calls to ask about a pending lawsuit with 7-11.

"OK," I say, "Let me get your first name and date of birth, please."

"Loretta, March 20th, 1943."

"All right, Loretta. Let's see what comes up for you." I shuffle again, this motion as natural as flexing my own fingers now.

The cards go down easily, nothing falling out of the deck. "I can see that you had a conflict with the company, but also a person on the scene. Did someone in the store create the problem?"

"Yes, a man filled two tanks with gas but didn't pay. Then the guy behind the counter accused my husband and me of stealing the gas."

"You were parked nearby?"

"Yes, but we didn't steal anything. The man had driven off, while we were being held in the store."

"But there's another problem I see here. Were you arrested or something? It looks like an issue with a man."

"Well, while we were being held, my husband has a massive heart attack."

"Oh my God." I throw a few more cards down. At least it looks like he's alive, but now my heart is pounding and I can't tell. "It looks like he'll recover," I venture.

"Yes, he lived, but he's very fragile. We're filing a lawsuit and I want to see if we'll win."

I gather the cards together and shuffle again, though my hands are shaking. When I shuffle this time, three cards fly out of the pack: The Moon, the Three of Swords and the Five of Wands. Major obstacles and disappointment.

When the cards go down, the spread doesn't offer much better news. "I'm sorry to say that you probably wont get as much as you had hoped, or that you maybe deserve. Your husband's earlier health comes into play, and that may count against you."

"He has been sick . . ."

"Can I help you with something else?"

"I just want justice to be done. And for us to get money for the wrongful accusation and the medical bills. They've been putting a lot of pressure on me, since he can't work."

I lay more cards on the side of the Celtic Cross. It's just not going to work, and I feel like shit for having to tell her. "There will be some money, but it's not as much as you had hoped. I would suggest trying to line up something else in the meantime."

"There isn't anything else. Just him and me and all the bills."

"I can see if there's anything coming in . . ." I say. But she's gone, like a phantom, into the ether.

Martin's astrology class commences after my shift, with just a few of us in attendance. Two people have decided to move out

161

of Los Angeles after the earthquake, and others just don't want to make the drive, with so many freeways and side roads blocked off. He's nicer than usual to us, and seems almost warm, if Spock had a nurturing side.

Again, we study the chart of the earthquake, almost like a tribe readying a sacrifice. As soon as we know what the world wants, we'll go out and kill it. In the meantime, we just have to figure out why it's so pissed off at us.

He points out the relationship of the natal Pluto in the 4th— the death of the mother energy, our respect for Mother Earth, or that strange, death-like vibe I feel all around this city. "Whatever the earthquake killed has got to come to an end at this time," he says. "Maybe the 10 would have collapsed and killed hundreds of people at another time of day."

"Or maybe we're all supposed to move on from here," Katie ventures.

"I don't think so. I looked at those charts last week, and this company looks strong for now."

We can all agree that that's good news. With so many businesses closing, moving on or simply deciding not to come back, jobs are at a premium these days.

Actually, we'll all be out of a job in a few weeks, but how are a roomful of psychics supposed to know that?

Two days later, we receive a memo outlining AstralPlanet's sexual harassment policy. We all get one, and spend about four seconds reading it over before laughing it off, folding it into paper airplanes and flying them into each other's desks. The office manager isn't happy with our response, but his one job is delivering it, so he just goes next door to deliver his missives to the employees of the sex line. That should be fun.

A few minutes later, Patrice ducks down the hall, ostensibly to use the bathroom. But when she comes back, she places a piece of paper on my desk and Katie's, pointedly ignoring Mercy, who's become almost like a ghost to us (except when she told us proudly that she had jumped into her car right after the earthquake and gotten on the 10 freeway, parts of which had collapsed, as if this made her poised and brave in the face of adversity).

I know we're back to normal when I read:

> This formal complaint is regarding sexual harassment.
>
> I respectfully like to complain against the unacceptable prejudice which [sic] is practiced by one Katie of the AstralPlanet Co.
>
> She neglects to sexually harass me enough to satisfy my sexual needs.
>
> However, it does seem that she does sexually harass others on staff.
>
> I feel she is prejudiced in her harassment—I demand prompt and effective dealing with the matter.
>
> I will accept as a solution:
>
> A. An enforcement of a quota of sexual attention to Patrice by Katie.

B. That Katie will be ordered to wear crotchless panties, spiked bra, 6" heels, black fishnet stockings and micro mini skirts (no long pants allowed).

C. That she will behave in a sexually provocative manner, drool a lot, and make loud groaning responses.

I appreciate your serious formal response.

Respectfully,

Patrice Bunzen
Citizen of the World

We giggle about that all morning, dancing around and making lascivious moves on the portable stepper between readings. The next time you talk with a phone psychic, imagine that we are people, bored out of our minds sometimes, and ready to bust down the walls of our cubicles if it means all the creative stuff of our minds can begin to come out.

For a few days, we become like the Three Musketeers, spending tons of time together outside work, doing readings, talking about astrology and arguing over Koch versus Placidus house systems. We're like the worst kind of geeks except that we have brains and filthy mouths. It's not going to happen between Katie and Patrice, but that doesn't stop Patrice from trying.

One day, we're at Patrice's place in Mar Vista when Katie suggests that they teach me how to trance channel. I've been using the Ouija board pretty easily since the first time I tried, and even used it by myself, but I've never tried to channel without the board.

"It's easy, Katie says. "You just push yourself into the back of your mind and let them come in. You'll know when you feel it."

She shows me how, letting her eyes roll back into her head, which looks more than a little creepy, and letting her head droop. Within twenty or thirty seconds, there's a different feeling about her, as if something else is inside her, animating her body.

Her voice is different, too, wavery and slower. "Zom," she says, and I jump, then dive for my notebook and try to get down everything she says.

"Patrice's fear issues can be observed through Alyson, who is slightly too fearless. Each member plays into the other energies, and the contact is productive. Contact goes in on subconscious states. Patrice has a tendency to project fears onto her environment and people. Her reality is formed by thoughts, which machines will measure some day. These are thought forms. She will not accept power or discipline, but attacks herself instead. She needs to discipline her mind and accept her power, and is close to the end of these issues."

Katie takes a deep breath and her head drops back down.

"Alyson is moving through a great change. The earthquake cut off her resources, and the past is coming back to meet her. It's like a compression chamber. It had to happen. The journey across the country was plagued by ghosts from the past. Her only clear desire was to achieve and work. Otherwise, there is a hurricane inside her. The challenge is to take the winds and control them. Make a stand here against the past and for your own future. You can identify the doors in the new places, and must overcome patterns of thoughts planted by those from the past. The future is one you never see coming. You will learn to communicate at deeper levels."

Katie is silent for a few seconds, her head bobbing gently. I look at Patrice and don't know what to do. She is watching intently, her pen poised over a notebook.

I'm about to say something, to ask a question or see if Katie wants to come back, but her head pops up and she smiles slightly. The skin on my knuckles bunches up and I can feel the air brushing by, cool and metallic, on the back of my neck.

"Alyson, the connection is growing in strength. You must continue to move more deeply onto the trance state we wish for you. To enter the speaking trance, where we will join with you and show you to better control visions, also we will begin examples of complex acceleration of reality to release you further from maya, Little Naked One."

Did they just call me Little Naked One?

I look at Patrice, and her face bursts open with laughter. Katie's face crinkles slightly with a smile, and I'm mortified.

Katie's head drops down to her chest as if she's a toy thrown aside by a careless child. It bumps against her breastbone. I can hear her breathing changing, becoming deeper and more lifelike. I try to remember if I've even seen her breathe at all in the past few minutes. I must have, right? But I can't recall with any real accuracy.

She raises her head and it's Katie again, with the same sparkle in her eyes, the same animation behind them. I'm sure my mouth is hanging wide open.

"Man, the entities think you're hilarious," she says. "Every time they get to talk to you, they all gather around like you're a comedy show."

Glad to know I'm entertaining.

"Seriously. They love talking to you. No one else talks to them the way you do."

I don't know; I just talk to them as if they were friends of mine. Maybe that's overly familiar, but I don't know how else to be. I've never been good at dropping to one knee and genuflecting, for much of anyone really. When I meet someone, incarnate or not, I just try to be friendly.

Patrice goes over to massage Katie's shoulders. They exchange some fake lesbian (in Katie's case, at least) billing and cooing before Katie turns to me again. I'm speed-reading my notes, trying to decipher the spirits' vaguely archaic and often grammar-challenged utterings.

"Ok, your turn," she says.

"Me?"

"Yeah, they want you to trance channel, not just on the board. Didn't you hear them say that?"

"I heard something I kind of understood, about going into a trance, but I didn't realize they meant, like, now."

Patrice chimes in, anxious for more information. "C'mon now, lovely. Then we can all show our tits."

I give her a look.

"I can dream, can't I?"

Katie sets me up in the chair she's been using, because it's bigger and more comfortable. You can slouch without disappearing into the pillows and I sit there, with my hands extended on the arms, having no idea what to do, or how to invite discorporate beings into my body.

"Just push yourself into the back of your mind," Katie says.

I close my eyes, duplicating what I've seen her do. My eyes move into the back of their sockets, rolling upward. I can feel them scraping toward the top of my head.

All of a sudden, Katie's voice sounds a little further away. "Just see yourself as if you're sitting in the very last row of a huge stadium. Let them know they can come into your body, then feel the energy entering through the top of your head."

In my mind's eye, I shatter into a thousand tiny pieces, blood, bone and skin fluttering everywhere. A hand enters, pushing an old fashioned broom and brushing the parts of my former self to the edge of a cliff. I see the parts of my body disappearing over the edge, and feel a dusty wind at the very crown of my head. It's like a thin column of something warm. I'm not afraid.

They tell me later that my eyes rolled all the way into my head and that my head bounced up and down a few times, like Katie's did. I don't remember much of anything until I come out of the trance, several minutes later. I do remember the images, which haunt me for a long time.

"Who are you?" asks Patrice.

"We have her," I say.

I see myself, even younger than I am now, dressed in shapeless clothing of a bygone age. I have no idea where I'm supposed to be, but it has none of the glamour of selectively remembered past lives. I am not a princess, and this is not my castle.

I'm being slapped by my jailers, and hear them telling me I've been imprisoned for speaking out about the king. They show me the writing I've done, seditious and stinking, and tear it apart in front of me. Adrenaline races through my body as I look down at my hands, which have been cut off, they say to stop them from writing. My hands are stumps now, wrapped haphazardly with burlap and tied to the arms of the chair.

Katie sounds way too far away to help. "Alyson, are you in there?"

I can feel my head moving about without my permission, but I don't know what it's conveying to my friends. With all my might, I try to move my mouth, to tell them to get me back, but it's just not possible.

My captors move toward me, several of them holding me down as they point to the walls, where I've tried to use my own blood to form characters, words, thoughts. They open my mouth and I can finally see why I haven't been able to say a single word in my first trance channeling session. There's a wad of cotton there, blocking my tongue, which they pull at roughly, using long metal tongs. I'm fighting with all my strength now, but four grown men hold me down.

Katie tells me that I start to make groaning sounds then, whimpering to myself. "All right," she says to whatever is holding me captive. "We need to have Alyson back now."

They cut out my tongue by hacking at it with an ill-sharpened knife. A jet of blood bursts from my mouth, splattering over my clothing and the wall beside me. It won't stop, and I can feel the blood backing up into my throat. I hack mouthfuls of it up, splattering one of the men holding me down. They stuff the cotton into my mouth again, but it's soon sodden. They replace it twice more before they let me go.

Katie's voice sounds a little louder now. "Alyson? We need you to come back now. Let her go, whoever you are. I command you to let her go."

The blood loss causes me to pass out, but I'm too frightened to let go. The men have left me in my cell but I'm already looking for something to write about. Even if this is my last breath on earth, I want to leave the truth behind. A little of it, at least.

Katie takes my shoulders and shakes me. I can feel that much, but my fingers are gripped tight to the arms of the chair.

"Let her go! Let her go!" she demands. Patrice takes my other hand, trying to pry it from the chair. "I'll banish you if you don't let her go."

They tell me later that my face forms itself into a sinister smile, like Jack Nicholson in *The Shining*, and I shake my head. Not letting go.

None of this seems like me when I come to. But eventually, whatever it is lets me go, and I come back to reality, panting like someone who's been swimming against the tide for several miles.

When Katie sees my eyes again, the concern on her face is visible. "Jesus Christ," she says, sitting back on her heels. "You scared the shit out of us."

My hands are there; my tongue is there. I tell them about the images I've seen, and they imitate the faces I made while in the trance. My hands are still shaking, and I can't write down what I've seen.

It takes about thirty minutes to calm down enough to ask them what they think.

"That's a past life, dude," Katie says. "You were some kind of fucking journalist, a writer or something."

Patrice adds, "But they sure didn't want to hear what you had to say."

"Do you know what time period it was? Maybe you can look it up at the library."

"I'm not good at that kind of stuff," I say. "I spent more time out of history class than in it."

Katie asks me to draw what I've seen, but my fingers shake so badly she takes the pen out of my hand. "I've never seen anything like that before."

Patrice throws the window open and even the bright afternoon sun is startling. The birdsongs seem cruel, the distant horns threatening. My hands don't stop trembling for an hour.

I doubt I'll sleep tonight. Normal, waking consciousness seems too ephemeral now, too easy to dispel with horrifying images and hulking, tongue-tearing goons.

February

✮ Aquarius ✮

I am curious, perhaps too curious.

For the next few days, I feel funny. Not like laughing, not like joking around. When they try to get me to dance on chairs at work, it seems silly, unnecessary, without purpose. The fact is I do sleep, more than usual, with placid dreams sent seemingly in compensation.

When I wake, my mind is calm, without my usual racing thoughts. My head feels heavier for what I've seen, and the knowledge of that day follows me like a cloud. I don't know whether to believe in past lives, and accept that I've had my tongue and hands cut off for writing the truth, or to dismiss it outright and go drinking. The latter seems so much easier and so I do, repeatedly.

I discover a bar called the Burgundy Room on Cahuenga, with pitch-black walls and dim red lights that seem to bleed onto the faces of its patrons. A mirror along the right hand wall bounces light behind the bar and back again, which isn't helping my vision get any clearer. The drinks, vodka and whatever's handy, are cheap and plentiful, and early on in the evening, before the douchebags arrive, it's a pleasant place to listen to some Johnny

Cash or Ramones, though the latter always makes me think of New York.

Speaking of which, I've had a few letters from back east, and the insults keep flying from my growing list of former friends. Seems my ex can't live with the idea of me existing without him, so I have to go through the painful process of reading about what a bitch I am from person and after person (who seem intent on reporting this news to me), or cut them off. Slowly but surely, I'm becoming alienated from everyone I knew back then. I can feel the flames of that bridge being torched behind me. I'm fine, I suppose, unless I decide to go back.

This guy with black eyes and frisky facial hair is sitting to my right, brushing his arm against my hand when he reaches for a drink. I look over and his eyes are locked on mine. Smoky eyes, with all kinds of dirty promises.

Someone puts "Ring of Fire" on the jukebox, and the bartender spreads a line of lighter fluid on the wooden surface in front of her. She touches an open flame to it and flames whoosh up, making our faces look devilish and distorted. Everyone roars with approval, singing along with Johnny's tale of burning, agonized passion.

The guy leans over, "Hey, I'm Alan."

I smile, drunk and stupid, not realizing what any of this means for my life going forward. All I know is the music sounds great and his arm on my shoulder is as comfortable as a winter coat, a cup of tea, a quick snuggle before work.

My head is sorry the next day when I wake up. It's up a few minutes before I am, bashing out a tocsin for all to hear. I'm convinced my neighbors must hear it, too, so loud is it in my ears. There's a rush of nausea into the back of my throat and then the blow to the center of my forehead when I meet consciousness. I rush to the bathroom and make it as far as the sink before I lose my breakfast, lunch *and* dinner, from the looks of it. The acrid tinge of alcohol in the air, the smell of smoke in my hair, and my clothes strewn around the room, boots over there, skirt balled up by the door. Please don't let there be anyone else in the apartment . . .

But after I clean myself up and scrub soap over my makeup weary face, I blacken a washcloth and head into the kitchen. Thank goodness, no one's here. I find a business card on the floor by the front door with a name, Alan. Yes, the smoky-eyed guy at the bar. I remember, a little.

Can't remember if I gave him my number, and there's little chance I'll actually call him. Not in a sober state, at least. So I crumple it up and leave it on the counter, checking to see if there's anything I might safely get into my stomach before my shift begins.

"Hello, this is Bronwyn. How can I help you?"
"Are you the psychic?"
"Yes. Do you have a question you'd like to ask today?'
She's whispering, and it's hard to hear her. "Yes, please."
"Are you all right? I can barely hear you."
"I have to speak quietly or he'll hear me."
"All right then, just let me have your first name and your date of birth, please."
"Clara, August 9, 1960."
"All right, Clara, what can I help you with?"
"You said your name was Bronwyn?"
"Yes."
"I just want to remember it, so I can ask for you next time. I want to know if I should leave my husband or not."

"OK, let me ask that for you." I shuffle the cards quickly, getting a creepy vibe from this situation. The cards go down easily enough, but I can't erase the dread I suddenly feel. And my nausea rockets back into my stomach, churning it this way and that.

"I can see that you have a rather dangerous situation on your hands. Are you all right now? Because I can send you to an 800 number, if you need help."

"No, well yes. I have to get away from him. He hits me and the children."

I take a deep breath, feeling my hands start to tremble. "Clara, I have to say that this situation is only going to get more dangerous for you. Are you in danger right now?

"He's asleep at the moment, but he'll wake up eventually."

"Alright then, I would suggest that you get out of there as soon as you can. He's not going to change and every day you stay there, you're in danger and so are your kids."

My voice doesn't even sound like me. I am clear, strident, in control.

"I know." I can hear her rooting around in a drawer for something, then the cracking sound of her voice as she begins to cry and blow her nose.

"Clara? Are you all right?"

"I don't know what to do. I'm in Alaska, and have to get all the way to California to stay with my sister."

I lay down a few more cards and am pleased to see that that's not only a possibility but a good plan, despite the distance. A few more cards, yes she can pull off the money as well, barely.

"Clara, please do me a favor. Get all the money you can as quickly as you can. Tomorrow, if you can. Then pack bags for yourself and your kids. Keep them in the closet. When he's gone, or falls asleep, just take off. Tell your sister where you're going and when, so she can keep tabs on you."

"Really? You think I can do it?"

"I think you can, and I think you have to. There's a new future for you and your kids waiting in California, and you can make it happen. The only thing to beware of is getting too run down, so you might get a cold or something. Bring as much cash as you can, so your credit cards won't be traced. You understand?" My heart is beating very fast now. I'm actually terrified for this woman I don't even know. I can see how violent this man is, how bloody he's made her in the past.

Clara stops crying, blows her nose one last time. "Thank you, Bronwyn. I'll be sure to let you know how it goes."

"You can do it," I tell her, and can only hope that's true.

When I end the call, nausea rises in my throat until it constricts. I ask Delia for a break and spend the next few minutes in the bathroom, puking up my pain and Clara's fear until it's all mixed together. Afterwards, I scoop four handfuls of water into my mouth, spitting out the rancid taste, and go back to work.

Delia's shuffling cards in her slow, methodical way when I come back to my cubicle. "Are you feeling all right?" she asks, ever the psychic.

"Too much of everything," I reply, as if that's an answer.

"Do you feel up to a reading?"

It's the best perk of the job, getting near-constant readings from some of the best in the business (myself notwithstanding), so I nod, flattered to have been asked.

I wheel over to her, gripping my cards in my right hand.

"I want to ask about this guy named Paul."

"All right, anything in particular?" I ask.

"Well, I guess where it's going?"

I concentrate extra hard because I love Delia, one of the least screwed up people here. She tolerates my hangovers, doesn't get caught up in office politics, and treats everyone with fairness. Cutting the cards three times to the left with her left hand, she watches as I take them back and lay out the Cross.

"I can see that you and he get along very well. You're partners and soulmates, in a way."

She nods, but doesn't say anything more.

"This person seems to be in and out of your life, though. Why is that?"

"He's a truck driver. Always on the road."

"Ah, I see. The relationship existed at a certain level for some time, and now it's about to undergo a change for the better."

I flip over the last card. The Queen of Pentacles.

"But there's another person involved. A woman. She's . . ."

"He's married."

I'm so flabbergasted that Delia, the one person I thought was above all the crap the rest of us get ourselves into, has fallen for a married guy.

"He's confused," I say, maybe stating the obvious. But I can see it in the cards, too. Going back and forth, loving one and then the other, sometimes both at once in his heart.

"She does have quite a hold on him. Even though he's away a lot, he still considers that home. Have you spoken to him about leaving her?"

She shakes her head, but from the way she does it, I wonder if she hasn't at least thought about it. "I can see that bringing it up right now wouldn't be a good idea. But he's more open to that idea in about a month or so. The good news is that he really loves you."

I can see tiny tears forming in her eyes and wonder if I've gone too far. "I'm sorry I don't have better news."

"That's OK."

"Do you have any other questions?"

"No, dear, that's all right."

I gather up my cards, and wheel on back to my desk. We're quiet after that, getting through another shift of other people's problems.

That night, I can't sleep for thinking about Clara from Alaska. I can see her gathering up her kids, making sure they have their coats, hats and mittens, carting cheap suitcases and meager provisions so they can make a journey to the Golden State. To a new life and freedom. I wonder if she'll make it exciting for the kids so they won't be frightened, calling out the names of the towns they pass, playing the license plate game. Most of all, I wonder if they will make it.

I try to eat some pasta, which usually calms my stomach, but all I can think about is how we all want the same things, to be loved and admired, to be cared for and appreciated, and how few of us can accomplish that without suffering and violence. After two more trips to the bathroom, my stomach is empty again. I like the hollow feeling it leaves behind, and go to bed early after an hour spent reading.

The next morning I'm on with Jemma, who's got the dress out. She's sewing angrily when I arrive.

"Hey, Jemma. That's looking good," I say, mostly because I don't know what else to say. I just like to stay clear of the bullcrap, if possible.

She grunts in my direction, barely civil.

I glance over at Patrice's empty desk. "Is Patrice off today?"

"No, I had to send her home," Jemma says, glaring.

I've never heard of a reader getting sent home, for anything. We pretty much do whatever we want, within reason. "What happened?"

"She talked back, and wouldn't stop fighting with me over every single thing."

"All right." I sit down and log into my phone.

She keeps digging her needle into the white satin fabric, arranging sequins and seed pearls with skill. I get a call soon after.

The woman is from North Carolina, and wants to know if two women "have anything" on her. I manage to get her name, Eulalia, and her date of birth.

"I don't think I understand the question," I say.

"You know, if anyone has roots on me."

I shuffle the cards, asking in vein if anyone has roots on this woman, though I have no idea what that means. When they come up, the cards are as jumbled as her mind.

"I can see that you're having trouble with these two women, but I can't see that they have anything on you."

"They beep the horn outside and won't get out of their car to go into my house," she says.

"Hmm, that's strange. But do you know these women?"

"They go to my church, but I don't know them."

"There's some more confusion around you. Does someone drink?"

"I like to have some beer."

"How much beer do you drink?"

"A six-pack or two every day."

"That sounds like a lot."

"Well, there's problems with my family."

I lay down a few more cards and see what she's talking about. Mental illness, lying, possible physical abuse. "I can see that there's help out there for these problems that doesn't involve beer. Can you talk to someone at your church?"

"I don't know. I never asked."

"I can see that once you've addressed these problems with your family, your feelings of being cursed will lift. There have been some traumatic events in your life recently. What are those?"

"Well, I lost my new white dress and I can't find it."

"No, I meant something bigger, like issues with your family, or money or something."

"Well, I did my wash and found a rock in the washing machine."

"A rock? Wow."

"Not a rock, really. More like a piece of a brick."

"Oh."

"Do you think they put anything on me with that?"

"No."

"OK, then, thanks. Bye."

God help me.

Jemma lets me take a break a half hour later and I hang out in the sun, not caring that I've forgotten my shades. I just don't want to be in that room anymore, on the other end of all that suffering. I'm leaning against the wall wishing I smoked again when Katie pulls up and gets out of the car.

"Hey you! Stop loitering!" she yells, turning the heads of some other office drones and the four or so folks waiting in line at the taco truck.

"Doesn't loitering mean you have to have had an intention at one time?"

"Shut up."

"Hey, Patrice got sent home for fighting with Jemma."

"Whoa! Fighting like punching?"

"No, I think they just had some pretty severe disagreement or something. She's pretty pissed. Just wanted to give you a heads-up."

Katie exhales. "Does she have that fucking dress?"

"Yeah, it looks like she's sewing her wedding dress."

"She gets that fucking dress out every time she gets a new boyfriend, and then when they break up she puts it away again."

"Oh my God, that's sad," I say.

"No, that's pathetic. There's a big difference."

I shrug, eyeing the truck. *Do I want food or not?*

"All right, then. Oh, hey, we're going to this healer woman in Pasadena on Saturday. You should come with us."

"All right, does it cost anything?"

"I think it's by donation, but it's probably not that much. She's really great and sees people from the other side, guides and stuff, and then she tells you what they're saying to you."

"That sounds cool. I'm in."

Katie throws her bag over her shoulder and heads inside. "I'll see you at the salt factory," she says. "Or is that the glue factory?"

"Oh man, you are dark."

"Look who's talking," she says.

There's a call holding for me when I get back into the office, and Katie is dispatched to the hallway to let me know. I bump into her by the Xerox machine.

"Call for you, Miss Popular," she laughs.

I pick it up. "Hello, this is Bronwyn, can I help you?"

"Bronwyn, this is Clara."

Oh my God. At least she's alive. That has to be good, right?

"Well, you were right. I just wanted to tell you. We left late last night, and it was snowing. I wasn't sure if the tires would hold out because we only have snow tires on the front end. Of course, just like you said, I got a cold . . ."

I can hear the sound of congestion in her nose, but am so happy to hear from her, I'm not even grossed out. "I hope you're taking care of yourself," I say, suddenly sounding like her mother.

"I am, thanks. We just got over the border with British Columbia, and I stopped to call my sister, so I thought I would call you as well."

"I'm glad you did," I say, meaning it.

She lets out a little laugh. "I can't believe it. I've been thinking about this for years."

"I'm so glad you're safe. Did you want to ask any other questions? I know this is probably expensive for you." In this moment, I don't give a shit if they fire me. I'm not taking this woman's money, the money she's gonna feed her children with later.

"Just one quick one, and then we've got to get back on the road. Do you think there's a future for me? A new life, as they say?"

All of a sudden there's a lump the size of Manhattan in my throat, so I put my head down and shuffle the cards. I flip them up quickly, to save time, queen, queen, page, page, and the Sun.

"I would say so. You've got a lot of cards that suggest a real growing up process for you, and assuming the role you were meant to play as a woman."

"That sounds positive." I can tell she's teary, too, and it makes it even worse for me.

"And I have to say that you have one of the most positive outcome cards in the deck, which means that yes, you have a very bright future ahead of you."

"What card is it? I'm just curious."

"The Sun. It's a card of happiness, fulfillment and light."

"The Sun," she says, musing, "after all that darkness in Alaska."

"Maybe this is your time, Clara."

"Yup, maybe it is. Thank you so much. I'll call you again when we get there, but you've been a tremendous help to me."

"I wish you all the luck in the world." I hang up the phone, in awe of this power I have done so much to marginalize, to *not* claim in my life. I've helped someone do something dangerous and succeed. And it's my gift that made it possible.

There is no part of me that doesn't believe she will be better, for once. I don't even bother to listen to that nagging voice in the back of my head, which says I have nothing but imagination back there. I've knocked it out cold with perhaps the best thing I have ever done in my life.

On Friday night, Katie picks me up in her battered Volvo station wagon, painted a mysterious mustard color not seen since the late '70s. I'm waiting on the curb in front of my building because you can't park for shit on the weekends in Venice. And since my street is narrow, I don't want people honking at her and spoiling all the good energetic stuff we hope to find tonight.

"Hey, lady," I say, plopping into a seat that feels more like a hard box of springs.

"Your street sucks."

"I know, but it's two blocks from the beach. I don't think they were thinking about navigability in a town built to resemble the canals of Italy."

"Can you read the directions?" She hands them across the seat to me.

"Sure." I navigate us to the 10 heading east, then up the 110 toward Pasadena. We're shooting past places I haven't been yet, so I glue my eyes to the horizon, where "downtown" Los Angeles suddenly looms. After the constant verticality of New York, where you have to angle yourself perfectly to see the sun setting over the West Side Highway, the word *downtown* seems funny. From the window of Katie's car, it looks more like 10 or 20 blocks of high-rise buildings that don't hold much of a candle to the Manhattan skyline.

"What goes on down there?" I ask.

"Mostly assholes working in banks."

"Banks? That's all there is down there?"

"I don't know. Drug addicts? Homeless people? Hoes?"

I make a face at her, concentrating on the road. "Then I'll have to check it out sometime. I love me some hoes."

We ride in silence for a few minutes, and I notice that half the road signs have been shot through with bullet holes. "Have you been bringing your pistol out here?"

"What?"

"Look at the road signs."

"Fuckin' hell," she says.

She crests Colorado Blvd., and we're heading north and a little further east, past enormous houses the likes I haven't seen since the Hamptons.

Kimba's home is modest but beautiful, a sage green Craftsman with original wood moldings, from the looks of it. We walk up the driveway to the front door, which is held open with a lit *veladora*, of Our Lady of Guadalupe. We move inside, where about 10 or 12 other folks are removing their coats and taking seats.

We sit around a large rectangular table almost like a weird, silent family, waiting in the semi-darkness for Kimba to arrive. I lean over to whisper to Katie, "So, what's going to happen?"

"She does some sort of healing ceremony, and then she goes around the table giving each person a message."

"OK, cool." I lean back, putting my hands in my lap. It seems more polite that way.

Kimba comes in a few minutes later. A large black woman, she oozes knowledge and power, not in a stagy or theatrical way but in the way she owns the space she takes up. When she sits at the head of the table, she looks at each of us in turn, kind of memorizing us, and then bows her head for a few seconds, murmuring to herself.

She greets us warmly, then asks us to join hands. I take Katie's hand on my right, and a woman's hand on my left. I can feel her pulse, swift as a bird's, through her fingertips. From the way it's fluttering, she seems scared.

Kimba begins to sing, low in the back of her throat, a singsong kind of chant. I've never heard it before but it's haunting and beautiful. None of this is living up to my expectations of being fake and silly, not at all.

She goes into a trance; I've begun to recognize the signs. She head drops forward on her chest and I can see from where I'm sitting that her eyes are rolled back into her head a bit. All of us are silent, eager to hear what she has to say. But she doesn't say anything, just remains in the trance for about ten or fifteen minutes, while we sit holding hands around the table.

When Kimba comes out of the trance, it's hard to recognize at first. But her head finally comes back up to rest on her neck and she gets to her feet to drink a glass of water. Gulping it down in three huge sips, she exhales heartily and starts with the person opposite me. "There is a person standing behind you who wants you to know that you are loved."

The man's eyes begin to water.

"I believe it is, or was, a woman, and she says that she still loves you."

He nods his head and covertly wipes his eyes.

Kimba moves around the rest of the table, and Katie nudges me in the ribs her with pen, impatient to get to our news. We're at the other end of the table, all the way around from the first guy, so it's going to be awhile. But finally, she gets to me. I have no idea what to expect.

"Your energy is very high. It's a bright pink/magenta color, the color of the heart *chakra* and the emotional body. You're a natural bridge between the physical and the astral plane, and a loving person. Behind you there is a tall man, kind of thin, with a black hat on. Do you know this person?"

I search my memory and come up empty. "No."

"Then he's a guide, to keep you safe from harm."

"Thank you."

"You're welcome."

Her gaze moves to Katie, who's practically bursting out of her seat. For a few seconds, Kimba just regards my friend in silence, neither liking nor disliking her. Finally, she says, "Either you can continue accumulating karma, which means that you will come back in another life to relearn the events of your life, or you can stop accumulating karma, which will get you a lot further."

Katie looks stricken beside me.

"Does that make sense?"

Katie nods contritely, squeezing her hands together in her lap.

"You also have a guide standing beside you. A woman in beautiful, flowing robes of pale green. She wants you to know that you are safe if you want to stop accumulating karma."

We listen to the remainder of her visions, then Kimba moves her hands around each of our heads and bodies, going from chair to chair and casting off any negative forces we've brought in with us.

She closes the evening with another chant, in a language I don't understand. I don't even try to understand it, but I know what she means. It's sad and it's lonely, like knowing what other people are thinking. It's filled with wonder and power, and a little regret, that this is what we've reduced our lives to when so much more is available to us.

On the way out, we thank her and drop our twenty bucks into a metal cauldron. I have no idea what's just happened, but I do feel cleaner somehow, released from my own doubt.

We're barely in the car when Katie lets out a long, "Fuuucccckkkk! Did you see how she totally burned me?"

"You mean about the karma?"

"Yeah, it was like she could see right through me."

"You think you do a lot of that?"

"Are you kidding? I *know* I do. It's just that no one's ever called me on my shit before."

"Yeah, nobody likes that."

She pulls away from the curb and makes that concentrating face that makes me laugh, because it's the opposite of how I experience her.

"You know what really killed me, though?" she asks.

"What?"

"She said you were the bridge."

"Yeah, I didn't really know what that meant."

"Are you kidding? You're so thick sometimes. You're the bridge between the waking and the dream worlds. You're a channel, a medium. You're not fucking around, you get it?"

"I guess so. I mean, I thought all of us were, a little."

"You are such an idiot. You get a huge compliment and you're acting like it was nothing."

"Well, if it's a compliment . . ."

"I'm gonna smack you. Basically, she said you were the shit. Are you happy?"

"Yeah, I mean, that's not why I went there, but it's always nice to hear good things."

She rolls her eyes at me. "You have no idea, do you?"

I look over at her, really not getting it. This is way over my head. "Sorry, but I guess not."

"I guess you'll find out then, won't you?"

My eyes turn forward again, looking ahead. "I guess I will."

I'm back home in forty minutes, and I've never been so tired in my life. The bed isn't close enough for me to fall into it. Maybe I can drag it closer with my mind. *Ach*, not yet.

Monday morning, I arrive for my early shift with Radar. He's quietly working with his bag of runes, so I take my seat and wait for him to finish. My first call comes in shortly after I log in, and it's someone looking for the lottery numbers. I hate these calls. I hate them with a passion. But I don't want to disturb Radar, so I say, "Are you ready to take them down? 12, 14, 19, 27, 30 and 45."

"Thanks," the male voice says, and hangs up. For all I know, they could win, right? But I don't feel right about it for at least an hour.

Psychics begin to trickle in. I don't recognize them, maybe because they work off-site, or our schedules haven't crossed yet. There are around 8 or 9 of them before long, and Radar asks, "What's up? Are you guys here to get your paychecks?"

One woman, with a halo of dark curly hair, says, "No, Martin told us to come in for a meeting this morning,"

Katie walks in just then, saying, "If he's gonna make us explode any more roses, I'm out of here. I'm sure I can come back in an hour."

"No, he said everyone has to be there."

I look at Radar and he looks at the desk, then us, then lifts all of his very tall frame from the chair. "All right. I'm going to find out what's going on."

But he doesn't get as far as the door before Martin sweeps in, carrying a clipboard and a pen. "Good, you're all here. Let's go into the conference room so I can tell you why we're all here."

Grudgingly, the readers fall in line behind him, dragging *Star Trek* backpacks and ill-fitting sneakers.

I ask, "Should I come? It's my shift."

"Oh, you can log off," he answers.

I do, making the short walk to the conference room and standing in the back, since all the chairs are taken. Martin stands before the group.

"As you know, the earthquake did a lot of damage to the phone lines we use to conduct our business at AstralPlanet. We were able to get most of it back up and running within a few days, and have been running at half strength ever since. Now, we find that the earthquake really did more damage than we had realized, destroying some expensive equipment and making it impossible for us to continue."

I'm sure my mouth is hanging open. I don't dare catch Katie's eye, either. Radar, the calmest among us save Delia, looks like he's going to throw up.

The curly haired woman from off-site speaks up. "What does that mean?"

For the first time, I can see that Martin would rather do anything than say what he's about to say. Eat bugs, date a Virgo. Anything.

"It means we're going out of business."

There's a flurry of activity, of raised voices and shouted questions. But all I can hear is the sound of my own heart beating faster. Since the earthquake, there are no jobs whatsoever. People are leaving Los Angeles in droves, scared of the aftershocks or sent home packing, just as we will be in a few minutes. Even crap jobs that won't pay your rent, like working in a bookstore, have 30 or 40 people applying for them these days.

What the fuck am I going to do?

I hear enough to know that we're not going to close today but at the end of the week, which gives me at least another few days of money to sustain my suitably less than noble tastes. A picture of the insides of my refrigerator springs to mind: mustard, ketchup, mayonnaise—a festival of condiments offering little nutrition.

Martin's mouth is still moving. He's wishing us well, complimenting our incredible gifts as psychics. I dart a glance to Katie and see the only flash of weakness I've ever seen. Her eyebrows are dovetailing at the center of her face, moving away from her bleached blond hairline. Mercy is sitting at Martin's right elbow, chewing her fingernails like a woodland creature.

There are no exploding roses, no clarion calls from the heavens. He gives us a few more days, and the shifts we already have booked. He promises to call us if a new line gets started from the ashes of this one. Apparently, this happens sometimes, or has to most of the people in this room save me.

Radar, Katie and I walk back to the office when it's over, past drifting psychics trailing patchouli and aromatherapy oils into the sunlight. I want to go with them and blink up at that fiery ball, ask it about what's next for me. But I have people to talk to, with burning personal questions.

Radar gets on the phone immediately, calling around to the Psychic Eye, the Bodhi Tree and other friends he knows, at other lines.

Katie buries herself in a book, more angry than hurt. I can't help but wonder if they've known about this for the week or so that we've been back, but decided not to tell anyone, when we could have been looking out for ourselves. Or maybe that's just me.

I don't want to talk anyway. It seems like giggling at a funeral, or peeing in a pool. I'm first up when the next call comes in, and happy for the distraction.

"Hi, this is Bronwyn. Can I get your first name and date of birth, please?"

"My name is Kasmir, and my date of birth is November 12, 1952."

"All right, how can I help you today?'

"I want to ask about a position I've applied for, at a local university."

Shuffling quickly, I lay out the cards. Lots of obstacles, problems with authority, the desire to forge ahead before it's really time. "I can see that you've had some issues in the past with your working life."

"Yes, most of the time they weren't happy with my desire to do good work."

"Well, this time it's more of the same, I'm afraid. You have a lot of skill in what you do, but the problems that tend to come up for you are based around personality, and the reviews you've gotten from past supervisors."

"Do you think I'll get this position?"

"You're certainly very qualified." I flip over another card. Not promising. "But I have to say that it's the wrong job for you now. The universe is saying no to this position so that something better can come about in the future."

"Are they jealous of me?"

I try to wipe off the smile that leaps across my face, reminding myself that I've just lost my job. "No, it's not really jealousy. It's more of a conflict in styles. You work one way and the person interviewing you works another. Does that make sense?"

I can tell it doesn't. But I can't fix everything. "All right, then, thank you," he says with a rigid, formal style.

When I hang up I look over at Katie, who's still got her head down. *Sigh.*

A few seconds later, her phone rings and she picks it up. "Hi, this is Katie. You say your name is Kasmir? All right, then, what did you want to ask?"

I have to listen now, so I make no bones about it.

She turns over a few cards and looks down at them, half sneering. "You are trying to work at a university? You have a lot of obstacles when it comes to that position, I'm afraid, and I can't see it working out that well. Do you want me to see if there's something else out there for you?"

She sees me and turns in my direction, making a jack-off motion with her right hand. I cover my mouth and look at Radar, who's still whispering into the phone at this desk. He's already told us about the homophobic dick stuff he endured when serving in the Army, so I'm sure he doesn't need Katie's actions right now.

"There's another position at the same college . . . sorry, university, but you'll have to be a lot more contrite when it comes to the interview, you understand? They're looking for someone who's a team player, not a lone wolf."

He goes on talking and she's twirling her index finger by her ear. My phone rings again, ruining my hopes of more shameless eavesdropping.

"Hi, this is Joseph. My date of birth is July 18, 1961."

I love it when they know the rules already.

"Yeah, I want to ask about my ex girlfriend."

"You want to see if you'll get back together again?" *Wait, his voice sounds familiar . . .*

"No, someone just keeps leaving these messages on my machine saying 'stop, it, stop it, stop it,' and I want to know if it's my ex girlfriend leaving them."

Wow, my greatest hits. I wonder if it'll be like this all week long.

I snap the cards on the desk, cutting them with emphasis and laying out the spread.

"I can see that you're both attached in an unhealthy way and need to stop all contact."

"You said that last time."

"That's because it's true. Did you want to ask about anything else today?"

Ah, sweet dial tone.

March
☆ Pisces ☆

I'm in love with someone who doesn't exist.

After the structure of the past several months, taking calls, being bound to a desk as if in supplication, at the very mercy of others, whose whims determine my ability to pay my rent or not, feels odd. None of us has time to feel sad, and our regulars just fade away as the energy is withdrawn from this enterprise. I wonder if Martin, an expert astrologer, saw this end in the chart he made at its beginning. I wonder if anyone else had any inkling of the sudden demise of our livelihood.

For a few weeks, I sit quietly at home, panicking. The want ads, in the *LA Weekly*, the *LA Times* and various local papers, are meager and, if I had chosen to be anthropologic about it, so revealing about the city I live in. Sex lines are hiring, experienced wait staffs (minimum five years experience) and real estate agents. How much has been left standing after a 7.6 rift in the earth?

Somehow, I have to find a new job, like *now*, to get me through this month.

But before that, I make everyone from AstralPlanet get together for one last send-off. About two-thirds of the psychics blow me off. Seven of them are leaving for northern California,

New York, Canada and North Carolina respectively. And a few just don't want to be reminded of what they don't have anymore. A reformed version of British glam rock band The Sweet is playing at a small club in Long Beach, and it may be my only opportunity to see them before they implode or I run out of money.

It's one of those beachside joints with pockmarked wooden floors and fake hurricane lanterns hanging from the ceiling. The opening band is breaking down as the six of us claim a family-style table nicked with knife marks and straight-edged hearts carved by drunken hands. A St. Pauli Girl-style waitress comes over to the table bearing an unsteady tray of beer steins. Tonight we're drinking for inspiration, so we don't resort to tears. Her boobs are impressive, and don't escape the notice of our group's male members.

I'm in my element, reveling in the tragic air of the place, the eons of history that seem to pour from the walls. It's as if we've always been here, wearing different clothing, sporting different hairstyles and voting for different candidates, but with the same impulses and the same results. Alcohol is making the uncertainty of life a little more bearable.

Applause signals the beginning of the main event. The new singer of The Sweet is a small guy with a decent voice, but his head is so small in comparison with the rest of his body that it looks like he's been Beetlejuiced. Katie is whispering in my ear and I'm laughing because none of it seems real to me. It's a play that's been arranged for my benefit, and I'm only taking part in some small way, reading my lines, laughing in the right places.

More beers appear on our table and I look around. The band is loud, banging out "Ballroom Blitz," and this music is making me so happy it doesn't matter that we're seeing a tragic version of a band I love. It doesn't matter that I've lost my job, that I have no money and little chance of finding decent work after an earthquake. Everyone else seems bored and anxious to leave, too reminded of their own situations, or too out of their element to care. They're depressed, and one by one they peel off and head out to claim their cars.

Katie and I are the last ones to go, making it almost through all the encores. I am smiling all the way home, but I can feel her impatience to get back to her computer so she can email her new lover, which seems to take up most of her thinking these days. Weirdly, it's one of the best nights in my life so far, and no one else seems to notice. Whatever's on the other side of this is a blank wall. But it has to be better than where I've been.

Five days later, I'm out of money. It's just the change I gather from the pockets of my clothes, the trays in my car, the junk drawer and pile up on the indoor-outdoor carpeting in a sad little hill. I separate out enough to get a few staples at the grocery store—to get me through a week, maybe, if I'm careful.

For an hour or so, I make a round of phone calls—to my family members, friends back home, and ask to borrow money. Even if each of them can only spare a hundred bucks, I can pay it back when I get a new job, which can't be too far off. It would stave off the terror of losing my apartment, or my life, if I can't feed myself.

But everyone seems to be in the same place. My family members want me to get a job, any job, so they won't have to worry about me. No one seems to understand that on a normal day, a good job would be hard to come by. A few weeks after a major earthquake, absolutely no one is hiring. Bankruptcies are skyrocketing, and every day, I see another business closing its doors for the last time, another pick-up truck loaded to bursting with furniture, suitcases, dishes and books, headed out of town. It reminds me of those dustbowl pictures Dorothea Lange took in the '30s, and produces the same dull ache inside. I'm told my family doesn't know what might happen in the future, and needs to keep all the extra money they have.

After the last call is finished, I hang up and sit on the floor, letting the tears come. No one can help me. No one will. Soon, my chest is heaving with sobs and it's all coming out—the months of deprivation, the fear of being on my own. Then I remember the tall man in the black hat—the one Kimba saw standing behind me, guiding me.

"Please," I say, "help me get through this. I need a job, and some inspiration and someone to care. I need money and food to keep me alive. I need friends who care, and a place to drag this terrible feeling of emptiness every day. Come on, man! Guide me already!"

For a few days, there isn't enough vodka in the world to drown the fear.

It takes a little more than a week, but the psychics rise again. Five of us hike up the mountains over Malibu, carrying the stuff of rituals. Mercy brings a thick plaid blanket, late of Tijuana, and Opal walks a few steps behind her, wearing inappropriate wedge sandals around 3" high. Her boyfriend Kyle and Kyle's friend Sam have a backpack full of colored powders, bought from a woman we used to work with, lighters and matches.

When we come to a graffiti-d overlook carved with the names of every drinker and dreamer in the area, Mercy spreads the blanket, kicking a few beer cans to the side. It looks like every spot where smokers congregate, where the burnouts and the ne'er-do-wells of the world come together, trying to get a little further out, a little less "here." While they set up the burners, I stand at the edge of the overlook, watching a pair of hawks circle and dive.

Sam lights up a joint and nothing about this feels remotely spiritual. Strangely enough, the worn beige cubicles of AstralPlanet provided just enough sensory deprivation to see into the future. Almost like an ascetic's cell, it allowed me at least to develop what I had. Now, with Sam getting high and Kyle breaking out a six-pack I had no idea was in his bag, all of this feels silly and useless.

We sit in a loose circle on the blanket. Mercy spreads out some green powder in a flat incense burner and tries to light it. A light wind kicks up, thwarting her efforts. Again and again, she flicks the lighter, without success, finally switching to matches when it doesn't work. Four matches are blown out before we lean forward, using our bodies to shield the tiny burner against the elements. At last, she's successful.

Opal's voice rises above the sound of the hawks' cry. She's got a lovely singing voice, and threads a light melody into the cooling winter air. The sky is still overcast, with low-hanging clouds that obscure any weather-related hope. When she's finished, Mercy says, "We're gathered together to ask for your blessings. Money, prosperity, opportunity and more. We combine our powers to request your guidance and assistance." She turns to Kyle, who's wearing a saggy grin from the pot.

"All I want is money. I need to get enough money so I can marry Opal." She giggles and elbows him in the ribs. This is getting worse.

Beside him, Sam cracks up, adding, "I need some cash, too, if you wouldn't mind."

He looks to me, and for a few seconds, I wish I were anywhere but here. Does this have any chance in hell of working out? We've talked about it briefly at the line, so I decide to give it a go. "If we're meant to go into business together, doing readings and sharing the profits, give us the means to do so, an endless flow of clients and a sign that we're on the right track."

The mound of green powder flashes up, sending a bright plume of smoke heavenward. Opal leaps back, giggling again. She seems to get this way whenever we're round Kyle.

"Whoa! That enough of a sign for you?"

I smile, afraid of pissing off the deities by adding anything else. At least one of us is trying to take this seriously, though from the look on Mercy's face, it seems like she's about to piss her pants. Maybe that's her natural anxiety peeking out.

Everyone looks at me. I don't really have anything more to add, but say, "Thank you. Please send the clients we need to keep ourselves going."

I turn to Mercy, who's literally sitting on her hands. She looks mortified, sitting in silence for a few seconds before she says, "I need money for my screenplay. Please send someone to buy it for at least $750,000."

I swallow, trying to push my feelings down. $750,000 for a relatively unknown writer is not likely. Not nearly. But what do I know? Maybe anything is possible if you ask for it.

The green powder is dying down and Mercy adds a little more to the pile, causing it to spit and flare again. The five of us look around the circle at one another, daring each other to have the last word, to direct the doings of the universe for our mutual good. Opal stifles another giggle and I want to reach over and smack her. This is serious, unless she has a secret stash of money we don't know about. No one has anything to say, so Mercy closes the circle.

"By the power of three times three, as it is, so shall it be."

She makes a hand gesture I don't recognize, almost like a fly circling a sugary treat.

The sky is almost cobalt now, as the sun makes its way toward the horizon, shot through with daggers of peach and slate. We're in the car, smashed in the back seat and winding our way back toward the 101. I can smell Sam's B.O. and the leathery smell of the marijuana in his denim jacket. Opal, sitting in the passenger seat, turns around to face me. "Were you serious about starting a business?"

"Yeah, I wouldn't have said it if I weren't."

"Maybe we should make up some flyers."

"I want to make sure you guys are serious if we're gonna do this."

She looks at Mercy, who's looking out the other window. "Me? I guess I'm serious."

Opal turns back to me, "We could work together at the Psychic Eye. That would be easier, and we wouldn't have to make up our own flyers."

The thought of sitting in a bookstore all day, hoping for people to walk in the door and having no control over that makes me depressed before I've even tried to get the job.

I shake my head. "I can't take the chance. I need to make more money."

"What about parties? We could do psychic parties."

That just makes me feel like a joke. Why don't you dress me up in a clown costume as well? Wrap a turban around my head and bedeck me in swirly Stevie Nicks regalia and wrists full of bangles? It'd be about as genuine as anything else in Hollywood.

"I'm not so sure I want to do parties. I mean, maybe every once in awhile . . ."

"How are we going to get clients then?" This comes from Mercy, who's not giving this too much original thought. I have very little desire to be in business with her anyway, after what she did to me at AstralPlanet.

Maybe this was a terrible idea. But the powder's flare—what did that mean?

Am I supposed to be with these people a little longer? Is it safe to depend on them for my livelihood? A cumulous cloud of pot smoke envelops me, and that idea seems more and more remote, until it's diving beneath the horizon like my hopes and dreams.

Man, am I hungry.

My little apartment, so bereft before, begins to take on a new meaning. I clean it more often, with more time on my hands, and take the time to get in between the tiles in the kitchen and bathroom, grinding the sponge into the gray-green grout there. How many others have lived here over the years, struggling with work as it came and went, with time stretching out endlessly? How many have dropped to their knees for the bathroom gods, the kitchen dakinis, their ways mysterious and eloquent? Am I cleaning off their grime, shed from their bodies in shame and sweat, in hard work and lassitude? And why the hell am I thinking about this?

I pop on some Ramones, the perfect antidote to thinking, but my apartment ghosts don't want to leave. I can channel on my own now, which I discovered late one night when I felt like I was tripping. With my fingers placed lightly on the planchette, it began to fly around the board, seeming to flip through my admittedly small vocabulary to find the perfect word to describe their intended message. Now I do it for hours, unaware of whom I'm talking to, which entity seems to want to communicate with me.

It's hard to picture them in my mind's eye. Are they white puffs of smoke, or invisible blobs like the Predator? Do they have my best interests in mind, or are they out to make mischief, as most ghosts are portrayed in movies and television shows? I guess that one in the *Ghost and Mrs. Muir* wasn't bad, and Casper seemed to be pretty friendly indeed, but it's hard to recall a time when the disincarnate didn't seem to want to fuck shit up in some way hidden from the rest of us.

There have to be answers for this next phase of my life, so I take endless pages of notes of mostly indecipherable stuff. They use names of people I haven't met yet, and timeframes and words I'm not familiar with. Some days I get so frustrated just looking for guidance that I sit on the floor like someone who's been lost for so long, even the idea of home seems unattainable.

In the weeks following the loss of our jobs, Katie has begun a fully-fledged affair with a new guy she's known for awhile. When we talk on the phone, she's distant and seemingly uninterested in things we used to share. She doesn't want to joke around or talk about channeling. It's all about sticking close to the computer, in case he emails.

I ask if Jermaine's fine with it, but it's still a secret from him. Katie's voice changes when she talks about her husband, filling with contempt and invective. "He's got to get a fucking job soon," she says. "I've been supporting him for so long, and fixing his teeth and all he's done is write a short story and occasionally clean up after the dog—when he feels like it."

"I've been having a hard time finding work as well. Has he had any luck?"

"Yeah, one thing. I might make him take a job as 1-900-TINA."

I cover my mouth, not wanting to laugh. "What's that?"

"It's a sex line, but he would have to play an Asian woman."

I think about her husband, a good-sized, muscular British guy, and try to picture him as a small Asian woman. But it won't come together in my head.

"Is he cool with that?"

She laughs again, a tiny twinge of cruelty in it. "He's going to have to be. He owes me a lot of money."

I wonder how she thinks their relationship will resolve, now that she's interested in someone else, but decide against asking. All I know is that now she's a different person, and our friendship is different. The person I saw as my buddy and mentor isn't there anymore, somehow consumed by a guy who's married and lives around 2,000 miles away, with extremely limited time to give to her or any sort of relationship. I can't count the number of women I've read on the psychic line, about this exact same dynamic, but it seems to be catching. Patrice has also begun to talk about a guy she left behind in Israel, now married, and the possibility of getting back together with him in the future. They've even found some other girls, also dating married men, to hang out with.

It takes around two weeks before I'm the odd lady out. I'm bored by all the talk about how this guy makes them wet, or that guy is going to leave his wife. I grow tired of hearing about how terrible the wives are for trying to stand in the way of these new relationships, and finally stop doing readings on when and how and where their new lovers might rush to their sides again.

The spirits become my new friends. They're always around, don't get pissed if you want to talk at five o'clock in the morning (any modicum of normal life scheduling has left the building since my job ended), and seldom have boring shit to talk about. They don't forget that you exist, which is a pretty good trait to have in a friend, and are attentive and available. In short, they're a lot more interesting than most of the people I know, plus there's that whole exciting period of discovery, when you meet a new person and can't stop talking about them.

We chat for hours every day, until I'm foregoing groceries and buying notebooks by the armload. I realize that as my friends are falling in love with real, albeit unavailable men, I am falling in love with a person, or persons, who don't exist.

Over the next few weeks, my schedule becomes something like this:

★ Wake up, smoke a cigarette.
★ Think about breakfast, more than likely blow it off.
★ Maybe eat a cracker or two with a Diet Coke, 5 or 6 if I'm really dehydrated.
★ Wash face or shower as necessary, then suit up in tights, a t-shirt and sneakers.
★ Walk for about 3 hours listening to the Replacements on my headphones.
★ Make my way down to Marina Del Rey to a spit of land projecting into the harbor.
★ Watch the pelicans for awhile, wondering how they get fish into their beaks.
★ Wonder if the pelicans get pissed off that their bodies make their lives hard.
★ Decide they're probably cool with it.

★ Make my way out to the very end.

★ Think about this being the very edge of the entire country.

★ Watch the sensations that arise in my body when this happens.

★ Know that somewhere, there is God, though I can't see him/her/it now.

★ Stare at the tourists, the walkers, the new families, and wonder about their stories.

★ Walk home when my stomach starts grumbling, covering the 2 miles quickly.

★ Try to get an idea, develop it into something worth writing.

★ Stare at the blank screen for an hour or so before giving up.

★ Think about how to make dinner from spotty ingredients and little cooking talent.

★ Read for a few hours, channel for a few more.

★ Try to sleep amidst the whispering voices in my head.

★ Fail, toss, turn and do it all again.

I am home when I sit with the board on my lap, learning to be comfortable with this new situation. The planchette zips from letter to letter, spelling out a message. There are no troubled feelings or sleepy eyes, no worries about paying the rent. My family slips behind me once and for all and even the fights I've lived through can finally rest as my mind becomes looser and free around the edges, untethered for these few moments of dialogue with the universe.

The world seems so huge in these times, exciting on one hand because all I want is to feel part of something larger than I am. I suppose I could join a cult, volunteer for some charity or stop viewing my personal reality as the central or only one in the fucking world, but that's all it feels like when the walls are so close. When I walk, I want to dump my sorrows and all the energetic shit that's followed me from New York into the drink. Surely the mighty Pacific can digest a little more human crap, transform it into something worthy and good.

On good days, I can see my way clear to having another relationship. My heart swells with anticipation of meeting a great guy, getting to know him and melting ever so slightly as we make some sort of life together. Will we marry and have children? Who knows? Having never had that phase that most little girls seem to have, drawing their wedding dress over and over, or imagining their life spent decorating a home, I've all but given up the idea of marriage.

Will we eschew marriage? Have kids? I picture us as a dashing international couple, jet-setting about, flying from country to country with our Patagonia clothing and sun-tanned faces. Putting our gorgeous baby in a backpack as her passport takes on another stamp. Taking her to more museums than she has years, and teaching her to read before she enters kindergarten.

This far down the road I can't see, even when I try. When the Ouija board cooperates, it tells me about a number of men who will enter my life, one after the other like a weird little dude parade. Who are these men, and where will I meet them? How can I just survive until then, with no jobs in sight, and no friends or family who will help?

More important is how I will manage to assuage the creeping feeling that I will somehow disappear a little more into my mind each day until someday, a person will open the front door of my apartment to find it completely empty. My stuff will be there, my clothing and dishes and towels. But I will be gone, evaporated into the ether like so much mist.

Soon, I'm channeling about four hours a day, writing down the things I hear, what they tell me will happen here and elsewhere. Images from the Polly Klass kidnapping sometimes crowd my nights, and even my dreams begin to be peopled with corpses, instruments of death and torture. Suddenly, I can see places in my dreams I have never been, and use road signs to help me locate. I can see the moment a killer meets his prey, where he takes this person to meet his dark needs. It's as if my senses are being wrenched open a little more each night.

I use my remaining hours to counter these black pictures. If I don't have a real boyfriend, I'll write him into being. I fill notebook after notebook with descriptions of what I want, detailing his qualities and goals, his looks, his talents. I try to create a picture of this man on paper, hoping that he will rise from it like Lazarus.

But time seems to move past me and often I fall asleep on the floor, my face pressed against the metal spiral of the notebook, a pen in my right hand.

A few days later, I run out of money completely. Combing my fingers through my pockets, there are literally a few pennies and a single gum wrapper. For a few seconds, I just look at it on the counter, not connecting what this is and what it means. It's as if the channeling has disconnected some crucial part of my brain, and shoved the meaning part, of which I suppose I should be afraid, back into some dark corner.

For the better part of two days, I do not eat, becoming pale and in my opinion saintly, as I do my daily walks (the gym membership has been sacrificed), channeling sessions and astrology lessons. By late afternoon I am swoony, and it's not hard to move out of my body to be cast adrift in the universe, unmoored to any space ship, without food and oxygen to sustain me. I wonder how long I'll last.

It's a Friday when I see the long black car for the first time, though I can't be sure it hasn't been here before now. I'm cutting across Pacific on the way to Marina del Rey, and have made it almost to Venice Blvd. when I can hear its motor behind me. Headphones on, I'm usually unaware of nearly all human and other noises, but the tape is flipping over on an endless loop of loneliness and drunken behavior. It's a bit longer than a town car, though not quite a stretch limo, with tinted windows the color of smog.

I push the button and wait for the light to change. Through the cracked window, I can see part of the driver's profile—a sharp, military hairline edged in black, no facial hair and a pair of dark sunglasses betraying nothing. All of a sudden I can't breathe. This is the government. They've found out about AstralPlanet's closing and are here to claim me.

Wait . . . maybe they caused it to close, leaving us alone and exposed. Fuck.

As casually as I can, I make my way across the street, forcing myself to not look into the windshield, to seek some further information about who's inside. Far from the usual Hollywood rubbernecking, I'm not interested in celebrity. For some reason, I'm convinced that my very survival is on the line. My body tenses, ready to spring into action.

Once across, I dart down one of the quaint walking lanes of Venice, which I know will lead me to the canals. No way a car can drive in there, and without a car, they'll never be able to catch me. My steps get faster now, and only when I can duck behind a palm tree do I look back to see the car sliding along like oil, coming around the corner in slow motion.

Today's walk will have to wait. Hearing a noise to my right, I startle and trip over a child's bicycle left lying on the sidewalk. My ankle twists, but I'm up and jogging. If I double back in a zigzag pattern, they'll never be able to find me. But what if they know where I live?

One thing Venice does have is alleyways, which make it easy to go back the way I came without being detected. I stick close to the walls, making my way through carports and trash bins until I'm closer to Windward. There's a coffee shop near the corner and even though it makes no sense, I will feel comforted if I can just get in there, maybe order some tea and get home safely. Maybe the proximity with other people will make their kidnapping plot impossible.

But no sooner do I step off the curb when the black car oozes around the corner, stopping right in front of the coffee shop. It's too late now. To go back would be to draw attention to myself, so I keep going, trying desperately to blend in with the hippies and wheatgrass crowd, the skate punks and Vietnam rejects. The driver gets out. He's built like a solid block of granite, with Howitzers for arms. And he's wearing an earpiece microphone.

After he speaks into it, glancing over his shoulder at a spot over my left shoulder, he opens the back passenger door, when a dark-tailored leg emerges, then the rest of his body. He's not an actor, you can see that from here. He's too pale and hard looking, not to mention a tad too old to pull off that racket. A politician, maybe, or government spook.

The driver holds the door open until the man gets out, closing the door behind him. They walk into the coffee shop together. In that second of deciding, I can't tell whether to kill time in the vintage store just beyond the coffee shop, or go down the other way, towards another alley. He's so close now, though, that I can't risk the alley again, not when it can accommodate that car. Once they're inside, I slink past the window in a group of people, falling in step with a dreadlocked guy carrying a dirty child and part of a garden hose.

In the vintage shop, I feel safe. The owner is friendly and there are lots of places to hide, if need be. Pawing through a trunk filled with scarves, I keep one eye trained on the door. Leopard, no, not today's mood. Red? Too showy. I make a small pile of acceptable colors and patterns on the floor until I can see the driver's footwear crossing my field of vision. The car door slams and I can hear the motor turning over. Yes.

"I just realized I left my wallet home," I say to the owner. "I'll come back tomorrow to get these." I drop three twenty-five cent scarves on the counter and make my way outside.

I can feel the heat of the coffee before I register his presence, but then he's there, the dark-suited man from the car, chest to chest with me, his coffee in my solar plexus. We don't exactly slam into each other, but the effect is the same. The springing apart, the apologies and embarrassment.

"Are you all right?" he says, looking now into my eyes. Is there a tiny flicker of recognition there, or is it my imagination?

"Yes, I'm fine."

"You're sure?"

"Yes, yes," I say, moving away from him now, looking left and right for the nearest exit.

"All right then," he says with a wink. "You get home safe now."

I am frozen to the spot until he gets in the car and they pull away. Then I race down the alley, running faster than I ever have for home.

April

☆ Aries ☆

I am (re)dedicated.

I can't remember what brings them to my door. Perhaps they're better psychics than even I realize, but Katie and Patrice show up a few days later, bearing two bags of groceries. I can't even remember talking to either of them on the phone, so maybe they've picked up a psychic distress call, or I've started projecting images into the sky like Commissioner Gordon.

On some level, I may even believe that.

Katie's first through the door, carrying a brown paper bag. "Dude, we were passing through the neighborhood and thought we'd come by."

I may be swaying on my feet, I may not be. After all, I'm not the best judge of anything right now. In fact, I don't know why anyone would choose to do illegal drugs when they could have whatever my brain is cooking up inside my skull. "Come in," I say, trying not to flinch from Patrice's decidedly frightened look. "Did you see that black car outside?"

Patrice hands me the bag while Katie crosses to the counter. "No, what black car?"

I try to sound off-handed, but know I'm failing miserably. "Oh, this car. Big, black one. I saw it earlier when I was walking around."

Patrice doesn't bother to hide her disgust. "No, I'm not in the habit of noticing black cars. Is that some sort of East Coast thing?"

Katie opens the refrigerator. "Play nice, Patrice," she says. "Mind if I get a Diet Coke?" But before I can answer, she can see that there's nothing in there but a condiment festival. I half expect the jars to go at it when I close the door, and give birth to a new slew of them every few hours or so.

Patrice has never been here, so while I show her around, Katie unpacks the bags, sparing me some of the embarrassment. The tour can't take more than a few minutes, and though I can tell Patrice is far from impressed, she says my apartment is cool. But it's not my apartment she's come for, I realize, as Katie breaks out the Ouija board and asks if I feel like channeling.

I look at it like a crack addict regards the pipe, feeling a guilty pang shoot through me. Should I give in to the urge, strong enough in me that my fingers begin to tingle? Or am I my own worst enabler, who needs to find a treatment program for things like this?

I plop down on the floor opposite Patrice, who's got her knee practically in Katie's crotch. Katie smiles sleepily at her and glues new fuzzy feet to the planchette so it'll slide across the board easily. "Are you trying to seduce me?"

"Always," smiles Patrice. *Doesn't she have a boyfriend somewhere?*

Then Patrice moves closer, places her fingertips next to Katie's. And I watch dreamily as our spirit friends enter the room once more, filling Katie's body like blood and viscous fluid. Her eyelids flutter and then she's out, back on the bleachers in her mind, gone from us. Her head bobs forward and she begins to talk. I can tell before she's even begun to speak that Carson McCullers has returned. The energy in the room is heavy and Gothic, dripping with honey.

"Have we been introduced?"

"Once before," I stammer. "That other time."

"I'm surprised you would go to all this trouble, Alyson. You seem to have life in a similar fashion to me—kind of a hard-living woman. We share a sense of beauty in the rough edge. Yes, I think your purposes are coming along."

"Do you have any words of wisdom for me? I feel a little . . . lost with my writing."

"You have the right idea. Simplicity is best, but I'm talking about stripping it down so that your characters are raw. Motivation is simple, like hunger, like sex. Even of a lot of complications accrete and layer over the basics, don't neglect the characters' relationship to the environment where their money comes to them. It is hard for you now, but soon it's going to be easy. Don't become frustrated when you encounter a problem. Just ask me; I'm here for you. Always focus on your first love, film, but prose will teach you, too. Your devotion and discipline can teach you in prose the language you need to have to feed mankind its raw truth."

I am shaking and close to tears when Katie comes out of the trance. But I play it off, yawning so I have an excuse to wipe my eyes.

"She really wanted you to know that," Katie says. "She's, like, really into the idea of what you're doing, but wants you to show how the characters' basic needs for security drive everything they do. In that one story you gave me to read, the dwarf was hungry—get it?"

"I think so."

But Patrice isn't to be denied, and soon they're off again, with Katie holding the earth energy and Patrice shooting off into the stars to bring us back some clues. I watch them but I'm not there. There are stories to be invented in my head, and I covet my time alone with the board like a jealous lover. They're giggling and flirting and before I know it they're headed down the stairs again, trailing insults into the Venice night.

After they've gone, I go the cabinets and refrigerator, to see what they've brought. Tomato paste, cheap pasta and blocks of hard cheese—nothing I eat. But I'm so humbled they cared enough to do this that I almost feel like Cousin Lymon, ready to protect whatever I've staked out in love, no matter what it costs.

After worrying about the black car on more nights than not, I'm ready to buy a gun. I can't afford one, but I'm walking southeast on Hill Street watching seedpods eddy around the Angels' Flight tram as it trundles up the grade and thinking about my ex-boyfriend's receding hairline when I make the decision to try.

After I left Lonny, he lobbied tirelessly to get us back together, often resorting to the crudest of ambush tactics. One night he emerged from a bush to offer a marriage proposal outside the front door of my building. When that had failed, he'd held a finger to his temple and pointed out the damage I'd unleashed, genetics notwithstanding. Before I'd entered his life, he'd had a full, *healthy* head of hair. Women had *loved* to run their fingers through it. Now he was a wrecked, raw man and balding to boot.

After months of similar accusations and the loss of countless friends, I've accumulated enough resentment to check out a local firing range. I vow that the gun will not come from any fear Lonny has inspired in me, but from the strength I've shown in refusing him.

It takes a week to find a firing range with a staff that treats me respectfully enough for a test drive, and an hour to try out the polished array of handguns there. A solidly built instructor named Bill rents me eye goggles and earplugs to protect my senses, then installs me in a narrow booth with hand controls for the targets at my left side.

Bill shows me how to load the 9 mm magazine, match it with the bottom of the grip, and snap it into place, forcing a bullet into the firing chamber. His chest expands then relents like a bellows under the shoulder holster holding a long-barrel Saturday Night Special.

He steps back, urging me to line up the Glock's bead with a spot below the center of the target. "Don't squeeze the trigger. Just increase the pressure with your finger, really slowly, until the gun goes off," he explains.

The first explosion makes my wrist snap back, then down to compensate. My heart is hammering. Bill pats my shoulder like any proud teacher.

The shot has pierced the center of the circular target. I am hooked.

After a two-week waiting period, I pick up my new Beretta at the range. I call it mine, though I can only afford to rent it for two weeks. Bill signs me into the unspoken union of gun owners. In the car, I open the plastic carrying case and stroke the blue metal with the tips of my fingers. As I drive, I think of glamorous Philip Marlow, then scold myself for conjuring such a romanticized picture of this killing device.

I carry the gun case past a new, dark-eyed neighbor unloading copious grocery bags from his hatchback and meet his gaze as he ogles me, knowing how much harm I can do. Before going inside, I scan the street for the low slung black car, just to be sure.

Inside, I strip off my skirt and stand before the full-length mirror in my underwear, holding the gun straight out in front of me like the fourth Charlie's Angel. I lunge, James Bond style, with it, squinting sideways into the mirror like Clint Eastwood on a bad day.

Over the next few weeks, I keep visiting the firing range, and soon get good. There is contentment in the instant just before the gun goes off, the yearning as sweet as the sore seconds before orgasm. It's Zen, a trance state, with no concentration save the animal sense of when is right, when is naturally meshed with the cosmos. The same fingers that can communicate pleasure can support a trigger, increase the pressure and make the thing explode.

Maybe it's a metaphor for life, or sex, or something.

Each time my finger coaxes the trigger, I imagine Lonny and his receding hairline. *Fuck him and his Rogaine ass anyway.* I'm in no mood for the fragility of men.

I am easing the natural tension of my shoulders down, going into my space, when there's a tap at my back. Startled, I point the gun downrange and turn.

He's a skinny guy around my height, dwarfed behind yellowish goggles and his own hefty eyeglasses beneath those. I look him over, one shoulder pointed toward the targets until I can safety my weapon.

"Hello," I say, uncertainly.

But then he pulls off the goggles and I recognize an old friend—Brendan O'Malley.

"I thought that was you," he drawls in the laconic way I'd almost forgotten.

Brendan still carries the energy of some older, cardigan-wearing joe from the 1950s—someone who probably sold used cars in the Midwest.

He's cuter than I remembered.

I embrace him, the 9 mm slapping his lower back. "Wow, Brendan. What are you doing here?"

His eyes fill with the same stars. Now I remember. He's had a crush on me as long as our friendship stretches into the past—the sultry days in New York, toting camera equipment and heavy lights. We joked and argued about music—his old band, the punk rock days. I'd pretended not to notice and instead entertained a parade of ne'er do nothings who'd called themselves boyfriends.

Why hadn't I taken him up on it?

"I come here all the time." He's also holding a gun—a Ruger 9 mm repeating pistol. "Can I join you?"

"Sure."

I reload my magazine and slap it into the handgrip with my palm. Then the safety is off and I'm aiming, very aware now of his presence behind me.

My first ten rounds are pretty good. Seven in the second circle and three wide. He snaps in a magazine and positions his hips squarely in the booth.

Brendan's stance is weird and gangly, almost awkward, and he scrunches his left shoulder up as he aligns the sights. He fires; all of his bullets fly wide.

He puts the gun down, his face reddening. "You're pretty good. Teach me something."

"I can't teach you anything," I say. "Firing a gun seems like praying to me. You close your eyes and just do it, you know?"

There are two beats of silence, then he cracks up. "No. I have no idea what you're talking about."

We fire off the rest of our ammunition, then turn in our eye and ear protection.

In the parking lot, he asks, "Uh, can I get your number and give you a call sometime?" His eyes are turquoise in the sun.

I think of hair care products as I write it on his hand. Brendan seems securely hirsute.

He phones a few days later to invite me to a gun show in Pomona. Though I can think of more romantic first dates, there's something intriguing about the idea.

In the car, he tunes the radio to some Mexican station playing oldies sung in Spanish. I watch his hands beating the steering wheel in time.

As we leave L.A., the land drops off to squirts of ragged, grayish-beige brush and the burnt remains of chaparral. Brendan points out the famous Pomona Speedway. "We should come out here sometime and see the drag races," he says.

"Sure, absolutely."

We enter an enormous, car-cluttered lot. He maneuvers the compact into a narrow space.

He gets out, notes the number and letter of our location, then shoves a tiny notebook and metal pen into his back pocket.

There are people moving toward the entrance, seemingly miles away. There are ten-gallon hats on five-gallon heads, bruisers carrying gunbelts studded with rounds of ammunition, and their big-haired girlfriends, sporting fringed white boots and frosty eye shadow.

Brendan looks at my blooming smile, barely held in. "When we're inside, you can't laugh, okay?"

I agree, though I've dressed in black leggings, a green t-shirt and purple Doc Martens. At home it seemed normal.

We near the entrance and wait in line to pay the admission fee. To our left is an information booth. A strident male voice booms, "I'm Jerry Adams from the National Rifle Association! Good mornin' y'all! Hey, you all waiting in line. Do you want your constitutional right to bear arms protected in our Senate?"

Brendan eyes me, testing my resolve.

"The president would like to see that right taken away and given over to the criminals. C'mon over and sign up here at the NRA booth. Your membership means we can keep working for you, to preserve your rights."

Jerry babbles this speech four times before we're hand-stamped and shushed through the swinging gate. Just inside is a dunking booth with a jowly, besuited Bill Clinton. Children taunt the silly-grinning man and wail softballs at the target. Everyone laughs or applauds whenever he hits the drink.

Brendan has his notebook open to a neatly lettered agenda. He brushes my shoulder to regain my attention, and I feel warmth ebb out from that spot like a pool of blood spreading under a door.

"I have to look for another magazine for my Ruger and a new Sig."

"Is that a nine millimeter, too?"

He glances up from his notes, a crease of confusion dividing his brow. "Yeah."

"Don't you already have one of those?"

"Yeah, but I want another one." He shuts the notebook with a glance of finality. The warmth on my arm freezes like a December puddle.

We round a corner to find a bank of about twenty safes standing seven or eight feet tall. Men and women buzz around as if they're hives, pushing their strollers inside to get a better look at the locking mechanisms. I wonder what they'll put in these safekeeping refrigerators. *Guns? Money? Jewelry?*

I can't think of anything I own that can't be replaced or forgotten. Maybe I'm not cut out for this apocalypse stuff.

Brendan pulls on my hand. Again I feel warmth move up my arm. We move into one of the barracks style buildings.

Inside, several long tables have been set up end to end. They're scattered with hardware of every possible description: gun parts resembling broken fingers, fist-shaped magazines, little metal bolts like errant jewelry and ammunition in every caliber. Leather belts and holsters can be embossed with desert flowers or your initials while you wait.

Brendan threads the human rapids, angling his slight body against the tide. Children are dragged through too-tight gaps in the crowd, sucking angrily at their fingers.

We stop at a table heaped with survival gear. Brendan speaks with a grizzled, desert rat of a man standing behind it.

"I'm looking for a Sig. Have you seen any today?"

I flip through a book on Molotov cocktail recipes. Articles on the impending race war are interspersed with crude drawings of huge-lipped Negroes and Jews with their hands in Uncle Sam's pockets.

I can't breathe.

The ratlike man blows smoke out between a hole in his broken teeth. "Try Building D. I think I saw someone in there with some," he says.

"Thanks." Brendan grabs my hand before I've memorized all the explosive's ingredients.

We pass more tables piled with survival gear, and I begin to wonder what these people are preparing for. There are tents, water bottles and purification tablets, even surgical tools left over from World War II—scalpels, suturing kits, tweezers, dental tools and mirrors.

It's a festival of fear.

At the next table, Brendan hesitates. I scan the pamphlets while he chats with an overweight man intent on the maintenance of his beer gut. His head swings on an invisible axis toward me, giving off a don't-fuck-with-me expression.

I pick up another treatise on the impending race war. There are battle strategies designed for specific areas of the country, complete with maps and bunker arrangements.

Exhaling, I put this one down and pick up a freshly printed copy of *Mein Kampf*. Adolph Hitler's idea of a good way to kill time. Brendan notices my curiosity and pushes my arm down until the book touches the table again. I lay it on top of the others and keep my hands at my sides.

"What? I'm interested," I whisper.

Brendan goes back to his conversation.

The table to my left is covered with Nazi propaganda: medals, swastika armbands, original German Lugers, and machine guns with perforated firing cylinders. I back away, bumping into a burly man wearing one of the armbands and holding a blond child in his arms. The child grins at me, ice cream and ketchup staining his little face.

Embarrassed somehow by the child's reaction, I cross to another table to finger through a multitude of videotapes dominoed together in a standing rack.

Brendan's hand is in mine again. "I think I found a Sig." His touch feels familiar. Warm, like a gun.

"I'm going to wait in line for the license over there." He indicates with his head and I nod back at him.

I turn my attention back to the cassette cases. On the monitor is a demonstration video of an oiled, bikini-clad woman rapid-firing an Uzi at the outlined figure of a target thug. Her well-conditioned muscles cradle the weapon while her breasts bounce with abandon. I can't help it; I cover my burgeoning laugh with a hand.

Another woman comes on, firing a similar machine gun but dressed in stockings, a garter belt and high heels with a bustier and filmy panties. Her body behaves in much the same way, her tiny heels trying to skitter out from under her.

I tear my eyes away from the screen to find Brendan in the crowd. He's seated with an amiable woman who's processing his application form while he scribbles a check. *Would he find the tapes arousing?*

I leave the video screens and rejoin him.

"I can pick it up in two weeks," he declares.

We walk outside, where a band is playing under a Budweiser banner. We get a soda and sit at a redwood-stained picnic table.

He's telling me about the Sig, how it's different from his other guns, and what else he wants to buy. I'm staring at a father who's feeding his infant son French fries from his fingertips, which are coated in brilliant orange ketchup like movie blood. An AK-47 rests against one shoulder.

I can't tear my gaze away.

"Stop it," he insists, waving his hands in front of my face.

"I can't help it. It's weird." My eyes come back to Brendan. "Don't you think so?"

"I guess, but you shouldn't stare. It's not polite."

Laughing, I swat at him with my hand. His mouth connects with mine right there in the sun and, though I'm surprised, I don't pull away. When it ends, I feel shy, as if we've just done a karaoke duet to "Sweet Home Alabama" or something.

"That was nice," I manage to stammer.

He fingers my tattoo and draws closer on the bench seat. "See? You fit in with these people. They've all got tattoos, too."

"Yeah, right. I have a weird clown standing on his head and they have Harleys and huge-breasted women. We have a lot in common."

"I was kidding." He leans over and kisses me, completely. I finger his soft, black curls.

"How can you take this?" I ask. "Isn't your mother Jewish?"

Brendan looks down. "I like guns," he grins. "And ignore the rest."

I scrutinize his face for signs of lying. "I don't know if I could do that," I say.

He takes my hand and we walk toward Building D. As we pass the band, I have a serious high school flashback. *Is that a Marshall Tucker Band song?*

Brendan buys another gun, which has me questioning his masculinity, and several hundred rounds of hollow point ammunition. The kind that's designed to blow someone's organs out their back. We find a spare magazine, then he wants something to keep his toys in. There's a table covered with black gun bags. A criminally thin man shows Brendan how to conceal almost any size weapon—in the small of your back, the front of your pants, or in one of his patented fanny packs. Brendan slings one around his slight hips, practicing his draw with the pack unzipped. When the guy walks away to help someone else, I ask him, "Why do you want one of those?"

"I want to be able to carry."

"All the time?"

"You never know what's going to happen."

A chill goes up both my arms. "Like, out there?" With my chin, I indicate the rest of the world.

His head snaps around to face me. "What do you mean?"

I fall silent.

He decides against the bag.

We're on our way out into the sun again and he asks, "Why so quiet?"

"I was just thinking."

"You glad you came?" His glance is quizzical. He pushes his glasses up his nose.

"I guess so. I'm just confused about why you would want to carry all the time." I skirt around a group of small children and lean in closer to hear his answer.

"Well, if there's an earthquake, or another riot, you never know what services are going to be cut off and what kinds of people are going to be in the street, or trying to get into your house."

"Who's going to get inside, Brendan?"

He shrugs, squirming, as though he knows the explanation is lame.

When my silence continues, he stops at a small booth, wedged between Nazi books on one side and an ammunition stand on the other. On several mirrored slats, in pyramid fashion, stand tiny glass unicorns made of twisted filaments and shining rhinestones.

Brendan picks one up and holds it out to me.

I smile tolerantly, just wanting to leave.

To the woman behind the counter, he says, "How much is this?"

"Four dollars."

He digs the money out of his pocket and hands it to her. She offers some crinkled tissue paper as wrapping, but Brendan shakes his head, refusing it. "Here," he says, handing me the glass figurine. "I don't want you to think I'm without sensitivity."

"Thanks, I guess."

My smile broadens to the brink of laughter.

Brendan bursts before I do. He grabs my hand and we're running for the exit, his ammunition banging against his leg in a plastic bag.

The last thing I hear is the NRA tape of little kids singing rap-style about what to do if they find a gun on the playground—

"Stop/Don't touch/Leave the area/Call an adult."

We grope in the car for awhile, kissing for our lives, then make for a phone.

My time with Brendan's fun, and we talk on the phone a few times after that. But I can't seem to let go, to lose myself in him completely. I keep asking myself what's wrong with me—I mean, he's cute, employed, not on drugs, halfway intelligent. So what I am, the Queen of Sheba, to be so judgmental?

Ironically, being with him, even sharing my least feminine interest of guns, makes me feel lonelier. Every time we talk about getting together—at the firing range, for dinner or possibly more, I keep seeing the faces of those children, smeared with ketchup and wearing the angry faces of their parents. I see them growing up like weeds, unhemmed and wild, slung over a shoulder like a handbag or a shotgun. Even trying to imagine him naked won't dispel the images. I return the gun, and that's the end of that little experiment.

At night I climb up to the roof and pry the aging lock off with a dull knife. I don't own a beach chair, so I spread a scratchy Ikea bath towel out and lie on my back to stare at the light-sprinkled sky. The slow rush of waves a few blocks over makes me anxious, and my mind won't seem to rest.

There is no edge to the navy scrim, no horizon unless I relate it to my own experience down here. But who am I? For a few seconds, I can't catch my breath. The enormity of space seems to envelop me, and I feel lost inside the darkness.

With so many millions on the planet, how could even be possible to find your soulmate? Maybe I passed him this morning on the freeway, but we were going in different directions. Maybe he left the grocery store ten seconds before I came in, due to a traffic jam in the parking lot. Or maybe he lives in Kentucky, or Calcutta, or Kentish Town.

Over the past few weeks, I've begun to feel connected not only to this new place but to people around me. Despite my lack of employment, my new tools reinforce the concept of connection in every moment. Tarot cards reveal what your subconscious mind is already thinking. Astrological charts are snapshots of your moment of birth. And my imaginary friends, made of no more than poufs of energy, keep me company when some of my friends are off doing other things.

But in this moment, I have to tear my eyes away from the sky, the sheer hugeness of the universe. Rolling to my side, I push myself up and stare at the tarpaper roof to stop myself from spinning. My own insignificance rushes up to meet me and I'm afraid I'm going to topple over the edge. My hand rests on my chest, trying to slow my breathing.

How rare it must be to find a twin flame. And how brave we all are, to go against those odds every single day of our lives, in order to find a connection so deep it transcends time, space and distance.

Will I know the right one when he comes along?

And better yet, how will we find each other?

May

★ Taurus ★

I am confused (again).

After a particularly strenuous hike yesterday, I wake up with a stomachache that radiates up my chest and across my armpits. Third and fourth chakra city. I've done no drinking in recent memory (can't afford it anyway), so a hangover is out of the question. Maybe I've lost all sense of nutrition, what with my diet reduced to ramen, tap water and the occasional cigarette. In fact, I seldom have to ask for them anymore. The guy behind the counter just slaps a pack on the counter whenever I enter the store.

I get myself together enough to be seen in public, and the same guy is waiting there with an expression that's so not there that I assume he's managed to direct his attention completely inward, like a star collapsing in on itself, while he seems to work for the security cameras.

"Ramen Lady," he says, when I enter.

"Yeah, hey." My stomach feels like it's filled with aliens about to burst out and rain blood and tissue down on the jars of Marshmallow Fluff and dust-laden cans of peas.

"Eight for a dollar today. And we have the chicken flavor . . ."

Is this as exciting as it gets for him?

Ah, fuck it. He's just trying to be nice. I grab eight packets of the salty noodle soup mix, some orange American "cheese" slices, a tiny jar of Jif peanut butter and two battered looking bananas from a wire bowl. When I get to the counter, I can see that he's got my pack of Marlboro Lights out. He's wearing a badge that reads Jamal and a not-quite smile that's as blank as a crocodile's. I don't know if he's winding me up or if this is his way of being friendly.

"Ramen Lady's total is $8.27 today."

I give him the cash—exact change—and he bags everything up. I get a little adjustment of expression, with the corners of his mouth moving a bit higher, but can't spend all day waiting for something that may never really take place.

As I round the corner, I think I catch sight of the black car, but it's a dark blue sedan with an elderly woman at the wheel. Though my heart begins to pound, I know it's safe to go inside.

When I get back with my haul, there's a message on my answering machine, a bright red beacon of hope. Maybe someone's gotten my resume and realized my incredible potential, or maybe someone needs help moving into a smaller place. Since the earthquake and ensuing flight from our fair city, everyone's taking advantage of the lower rents or moving in with friends and family members to save money.

But Katie's voice comes out when I push play. "Hey weirdo, what's going on? I got a call from Delia and she was wondering how you're doing. She wants to get together next week for coffee or something at her place in Toluca Lake. Anyway, call me back!"

But she's lost me at "weirdo." I don't know why, but the word stings. I've spent my life first doing everything I could to be different—wearing thick black eyeliner, thrift store clothes and reading *Ulysses* in study hall until I got in trouble for reading a banned book (don't ask)—but now that there's been a natural disaster, I'm trying to fit in. Scratch that. I feel like I *have* to fit in. Maybe it's the human tendency to hang with the pack when survival is at issue, I have no idea, but I've imagined a Donner Party situation on more nights than not, with George Romero-style zombies busting storefront windows on Abbott Kinney and making their way to the beach houses to forage for frozen candy bars and canned goods.

They say I'm a psychic, so I guess that means I'll never fit in. I wish I could let all this roll off my back and be cooler than shit about it. And maybe with time that'll be the case. But for now I have to be comfortable with the fact that maybe I am a weirdo.

I pick up the phone, dial it and then I'm joking around with Katie and for a few seconds I forget what she called me and why I was upset about it. I get in a few well-intentioned insults and tease her about her affair with the married guy. My life seems calm and almost normal in comparison, unless you consider the plethora of imaginary friends and complete lack of funds to, I don't know, feed myself on a daily basis.

We meet at Delia's six days later, at a tiny condo complex north of Pass Ave. in Toluca Lake. It's hidden on all sides with lush greenery that almost manages to conceal the fact that the units are small and placed just yards from the 134 Freeway. She's smiley and serving up tea in actual china cups when we arrive. The fact that she's wearing an apron isn't lost on me. For many of us, she seemed like the mom of the group, a calm oasis in the midst of the insanity.

When the tea is gone, we're catching up and laughing about the other psychics we've worked with, some of whom have scattered to other lines or started their own businesses. One is going to massage school, and several have left town for parts unknown. Of these, two have plans to open metaphysical bookstores in small towns, hoping that the lack of competition will keep them in business. I can only hope that there are no shifting tectonic plates to scuttle their plans.

As with most psychic gatherings, there are readings. Delia reads Katie first, asking if the guy she saw a few months earlier has shown up to test her marriage. Katie smiles a guilty little number, and I plaster my mouth shut. Delia knows, though. I can see it on her face.

"He might have," Katie says. Delia is the only one who can reduce her to this childlike state. At least when she's not planning something of her own, or trying to get something.

Delia lays out a few more cards and puts her chin on her hand. "I can see that this is a long-lasting relationship, and it's really up to the two of you to take it where you will."

Katie looks at her with wide eyes.

"And I wouldn't really worry about the wife. She knows that he's done this before, and won't be around forever."

Now Katie looks mortified, but this is why I love Delia. Why everyone loves her. She's so great at what she does, yet so wonderful about how she can deliver the news that you don't hate her for seeing right inside your head. Because even though most people think they want to find out about the future, they really don't. They want to hear what they want to hear. It takes guts to find out what's really going to happen, if you keep going in the same direction, and to become truly responsible for the paths we forge on a daily basis.

It's my turn next. "What do you want me to focus on?" she asks.

It's the same old thing. The same old question. And I am embarrassed to have to keep asking it. As if everyone else has been handed the manual for living, and I missed class that day. But you never get anywhere by not asking. "All right," I say. "I'm on the verge of giving up men, switching to the other team or entering a nunnery. The guys I seem to meet are all . . ."

"That should be enough." She's already shuffling, whirring the magical oracles together like tiny fortunetelling soldiers. I even like the way she lays out the cards, all smooth and intentional, instead of chaotically snapping the cards down, like I do.

I have to resist the urge to read the cards myself, upside down, and realize it's like going to a movie after you've been to film school. You know how it's done and have to suspend your disbelief even more than before, shoving your conscious self back into a corner and letting it be. Delia takes a few moments with the cards, letting them seep into her consciousness.

"There are a few guys out there, two of them I'm seeing now. But neither one of them lives here . . ."

"Figures." Katie shoots me a dirty look, like she has any say here.

"I can see that it's somewhere up north, maybe San Francisco or Portland, and one of them has a daughter."

"A daughter?"

"Yeah, you're going to date one of them, and then the other, and I think the second one's going to work out."

She stares at the cards a few more seconds before declaring, "But you have to get yourself out there more."

Out there? What am I, a spaceship? I don't know how I could be any more out there without literally putting my face and vital stats on a billboard.

"I don't know what you mean."

She sits back on the couch, looking like a tropical bird on a beige chenille branch, appraising me with those all-seeing eyes.

"When's your birthday again?"

"December."

"It's already passed."

"Yup."

"You know what? I'm going to get you a birthday present."

I feel a red flush creeping across my cheeks. Katie's almost glaring at me. She's gotten no such gift from Delia. "You don't have to do that," I say.

"No, I want to. I'm going to get you a personal add in the *L.A. Weekly*. Ever read the personals in the back?"

"Not really."

She and Katie exchange a look. A sly smile slides across Katie's features. I want to slap her.

Delia says, "It's perfect, actually. You place an add, they send you pictures and a note, and you can choose which ones you go out with."

My face must be twisting itself into mortified shapes, because Katie bursts out laughing, then eggs Delia on. "Do it; do it. Look at her!"

Why do I hate her so much right now?

A few days later, I receive a letter from Delia, along with an application for the personal ad. I've never done this before, and have no frame of reference save for those scenes in *Desperately Seeking Susan* where Madonna's boyfriend is trying to find her, and that bears no resemblance to my life now. There are little blanks to fill in, with 25 spaces available.

How does one go about advertising for love? Should I promote my best qualities, or create a list of what I'm seeking? The whole thing seems like a lot of work.

But after dinner, another packet of ramen and my fifth cigarette of the day, I'm stretched out on the floor, bored out of my skull. I can see a jagged crack in the ceiling, a remnant of the earthquake, and wonder how safe our building really is. Then I flip over onto my stomach and coax a notebook open with my fingertips. Even the indoor-outdoor carpeting smells like salt water.

I play with words on the pad, crumpling several pages before I find a combination I can live with. It's like writing the least successful haiku in history:

> Not particularly attractive girl seeks same (but of
> the male persuasion) for fun and games. Must like
> toe jam, long walks, pelicans and ramen.

To my mind it's so destined to fail that I can't possibly hurt Delia's feelings. No one's going to respond; no way in hell. Famous last words.

About a week later, the mailman leaves me a thick manila envelope stuffed with smaller, letter-sized envelopes. I spill them out on the floor, arranging photos next to letters until I have 10 or 12 of them. Really?

The thing is, they sound like nice enough dudes. It would be well enough if I could moralize and feel superior to them, dismiss them as so much pathetic detritus in a loveless world, but I can't. Seven of them have been drawn in by the humor in my ad, two seem to have responded to everyone listing anything at all (the form letter is a dead giveaway), and three appear to have been educated under the nearest tree stump. The salesmanship of this endeavor can't be underestimated, and I am a bit stunned to realize, in one prolonged instant, that all of us are doing this, all the time.

I don't know how Delia knows, actually I do, but she calls me the next day to ask about the responses to my ad. Busted, I can't back out of it, not convincingly at least, and am forced to admit that there have been twelve so far.

"Any of them cute?" she asks. I can hear her smile traveling through the line.

I page through the ones that have made the preliminary cut. None of them is going to win a beauty contest anytime soon, but more than a few of them are palatable enough. Maybe my standards need raising, or I'm just a bit more tolerant than the average L.A. lady.

"Yeah, there are a few . . . um, interesting ones."

"You never know. Maybe one of them could surprise you."

"I'm not promising anything," I say, already trying to back out of it.

Delia laughs. "We're all well aware of your stubbornness, but think of it as an adventure, a door to walk through. Maybe you'll walk through it and it'll take you to a brand new place, right?"

I can't argue with her, as usual. "I'll let you know how it goes."

I respond to a guy named Keith, in part because he shares a moniker with one of my favorite rock stars. There's a picture of him over my desk (the rock star, that is), wearing a towel on his head and a t-shirt reading "Who the fuck is Mick Jagger?" It reminds me to never take the world too seriously, so it's with this same dive-in-and-see-what-happens attitude that I call him and leave a message.

My daily walks are getting longer and longer as I get broker and broker. I'm smoking more, too, convinced on some level that smoking's not bad for me. Maybe the walking is offsetting the lung-closing properties of tobacco. But more than one of my friends has expressed worry about my sanity when I tell them of my experiences.

My legs have stopped hurting as I push beyond what I can feel. Maybe my body disappears entirely. I can't be sure. But now that I have all the time in the world, I'm uninterested in writing. Cruelly, the ideas keep coming, one better than the next, for stories, screenplays, novels and more. I feel duty bound to scratch down a few notes about them, in the hopes that this mental exile will end soon. All I can dream about is a new love, which will take me past anything I've ever experienced before. Not in the Harlequin novel kind of way, but in a manner that surprises and delights.

Despite all signs to the contrary, I feel that I'm being guided, though I'm not sure why. I've never felt that way in my life before, more like its opposite, as events around me seemed to conspire to make me unhappy and unfulfilled. But what if that could be different? What if there really was a way to break out of your past and become someone brand new?

As I walk, I practice the astrological aspects in my mind until I memorize them:

> **Conjunctions** are like love, with two planets coming so close to each other that they could almost kiss in the sky.

Sextiles are like friendships, with communication, harmony and shared interests but not enough spark to make them romantic.

Trines are like friends with benefits, where two energies get along so well and it's so easy that little action is required to bring them together. The challenge lies in keeping them there.

Squares are like the characters in *Who's Afraid of Virginia Woolf?,* too dug into their respective positions to get along, yet too attached to get away from the source of their pain.

Oppositions are like old married couples, where two planets are pulling in opposite directions, but need the other to balance their thrust into the universe.

I look for the long black car again and again, but never see it. I don't know whether to be relieved or worried anew. Over and over I repeat the aspects in my brain until they're as imprinted as childhood memories. There are applying aspects, where planets are moving toward each other, growing stronger with each day, and separating aspects, where their influence diminishes and wanes. My unnamed guy, out there in the ether, is applying or separating? Have we already had our conjunction, at some earlier time, or is this still to come, when the planets are damned good and ready?

Six days later, I meet Keith of the *L.A. Weekly* personal ad, in a West Hollywood coffee shop. I hate coffee with a passion, and never know what to order in these places. But it seems like a rite of passage, the first "coffee" date, where alcohol won't influence your senses and lead to an all-too-quick and disastrous sexual encounter, so I comply. A little.

I wait toward the back, on a purple velvet couch that makes me feel like an 18th century hooker. The swirly blue patterns on my vintage skirt clash with the décor and all of a sudden I'm panicking about what I've worn and the makeup I've chosen and even the decision to be here in the first place. I am notoriously bad at lying, at pretending I'm having a good time when I'm not, that on more than one occasion in the past, I've stayed longer, stammered and made an ungraceful exit then hated myself for hours afterwards. I hope this afternoon won't be one of those times.

I order and pay for a carrot muffin and mango juice, staying in the orange food group, and then I see him pushing the door open with a semi-mortified expression on his face. Maybe he's as terrified as I am, to try out this seemingly unwinnable thing.

"Keith," I say, when he gets closer. "I'm Alyson."

He lets a grin break over his face. "Alyson!"

Keith sinks down next to me on the purple sofa and I can sense his relief, at my being here, at not having to break the ice himself. If I wanted to, I could look inside his head, I know that now, but part of me doesn't want to deny him his privacy, or ruin the surprise. "I'm gonna get a coffee," he says, leaping up and moving the few steps to the counter.

I look around the place—a few hipsters staring into laptops, devoid of ideas, one older guy seemingly in the wrong place, and a French actress from a few local indies. She's even beautiful in person, *sans* makeup. Then he's back at my side, balancing a sturdy mug and a pastry, dropping crumbs. "You got a table; that's good. Sometimes, I have to stand at the counter, or sit in one of those metal chairs outside. But it's hot out there, and . . . anyway, I'm babbling."

I sip my juice. "No, you're fine," I say. "It's nice to meet you."

"You, too. He you ever done anything like this before?'

"No, never. My friend bought the ad for me. What about you?"

"I met one girl through an ad, and she was nice. But then she moved to Ojai, so I never saw her again."

I wonder if "moving to Ojai" is slang for "I don't know how to tell you I never want to see you again," but decide to not mention this, in the spirit of kindness. "It's kind of weird, isn't it?"

Again, he seems relieved, and I'm almost beginning to like this Keith dude named after one of my favorite rock stars. He seems like a nice guy, a regular guy with few needs and simple ways. Someone who dreams not in color but in black and white, just like *It's a Wonderful Life*, which is probably his all-time favorite movie. But I like them complicated, with a mile-wide dark streak and a sense of humor to match. I like sweetness inside the swagger, and a devilish twinkle.

And it goes without saying that when the coffee and juice are drunk, as the last crumbs of baked goods are gathered on tongue-wettened fingers, I'm just not attracted to this wonderful guy who's clearly meant for someone else. Maybe I should have asked to see his chart first. But that kind of stuff tends to creep out even the nicest of people.

We say goodbye and I am cringingly aware that he's trying to figure out how to kiss me, where to do it, when to make the eventual call. But I take his hand when we're outside, look deeply into his eyes and blurt, "You're a really nice guy . . ."

He's surprised that I've scooped him, and stammers back, "Yes, I mean you. You're really nice, too . . . no toe jam at all, I gather."

I don't break eye contact. ". . . but I've just gotten out of a bad relationship . . ."

"Oh?" His confidence is starting to flag. I am such a huge, inflated donkey dick right now.

". . . a really bad relationship . . . bad breakup . . . and I just don't know if I'm ready to move into anything new now."

Keith looks less like a rock star than ever before. He says, "Do you want to just take it slow for now, get to know each other?"

"Let me do this. I have your number, so let me see how I feel in a few days and maybe we can talk on the phone, all right?"

I leave him on the West Hollywood sidewalk, blinking in the sun. He has no idea what's hit him, and neither do I. I'm like a meteor raining down from a bloody sky, leaving mango juice and the scent of honeysuckle in my wake. I have no intention of calling, but I can't tell him that. My soul feels a little smaller, a little less alive, as I walk to my car and key the door open. No amount of cool air on my face will drive the feeling away.

I have no idea how guys do this on a regular basis. It's like having all the best parts of you cut away, without anesthesia.

Money is calling the loudest, beating a resounding *fuck you* in my brain. It's my first thought every day when I wake up, and the last thing I think about before I fall asleep. How long can someone go without funds, I wonder? How long can the inevitable departure from the socially contrived notion of home be put off?

But somehow I make it, patching together small amounts of money from family and friends, a few dollars here and there from readings I do on my own, and even cash I find while walking on the beach. That's probably the last time anyone has been paid for that particular activity. But I'm not exactly getting rich quick, and am further from supporting myself with every day that passes.

A few days later, I'm talking to Sylvie, a friend from film school who's moved out to Los Angeles to pursue a career in screenwriting, on the phone. Bitching about my lack of funds, as usual. I sound like every whining asshole who thinks the world owes them a living, except that I'm living in a town that doesn't care that I have ten years of writing and editing experience, nor that there's just been a devastating earthquake. Landlords have this crazy notion that you should keep paying them anyway. Bastards.

Probably to get me to shut up, she says, "Why don't you temp?"

I've never even considered that; I don't even know how to type. Here, the closest thing to New York-looking office buildings are clustered in that tiny area called "downtown," which I have no idea how to get to. Is that where all the temps work?

"We do it sometimes when we need money. Sometimes Tom temps while I write, and sometimes I do it so he can write."

"What does it pay?"

"It depends on where you get placed. Tom usually works at Disney, and they pay twelve bucks an hour."

That sounds like a fortune to me. I have images of myself rolling in an endless green sea of money, then realize I have to be serious. "That's pretty good. But how do you get the jobs? Did you have to go to Disney or something?"

"No, it's really simple. You sign up with an agency or two, and then they find jobs for you."

Fuck, really? What have I been trying to do for the past three months like an idiot?

She gives me the names and numbers of the two agencies that have found them the most work, and says I can use Tom's name. I have no idea what to expect and feel so ground down by the months of craziness and poverty that for a moment I'm not sure I can pick up the phone and have a regular conversation with another adult. At least not one who knows me and has made concessions for my idiosyncrasies.

But one look into the refrigerator pushes me back to my desk. I pick up the phone and dial it quickly, before I can change my mind.

"Right Connections," a female voice says.

"Hi," I manage. "I'd like to find out how I might go about temping with you."

The next day, I dress up in my best clothes (no need to comment on that), and make my way over to La Cienega for an interview. Two hilarious women run the agency, amidst cats, paper-laden desks and a host of desperate looking youngsters in the waiting room. One of them has actual cats-eye glasses that she's definitely had on her head since the '50s, and a hairstyle that would frighten Phyllis Diller. I can tell from their accents that they're originally from New York, or somewhere on the East Coast, so I feel instantly and completely at home, despite my allergy to cats.

"How fast can you type?"

"Uh, probably around 45-50 words per minute," I lie.

"Any other skills?"

"Sure. I was a writer and editor for several New York publishing houses. I've worked in film and TV production . . . uh . . ."

"That's fine," one of them says, noting everything on a coffee-stained pad. "Do you have a suit?'

"No, not at the moment."

"You should get a suit. It looks professional."

To temp in? For twelve bucks an hour?

"I can look into that."

"Good. How are you at answering phones?'"

It can't be hard, can it? You just pick up the receiver and say something . . .

"I can answer phones," I say, trying for perky career girl on the go.

"Then I think I may have something for you."

Luckily, my first day is at a post-production house in Hollywood, where I'm placed in front of an enormous bank of phones, probably 30 lines or so, at 8:30 the next morning. My best clothes are apparently good enough, because I don't get any weird looks or comments. Truth be told, I can barely keep my eyes open at this hour. I've never been much of a morning person. Receptionist work pays only ten dollars per hour, but I'm grateful for even that much.

I'm answering phones for eleven people, all of whom want their phone picked up after a specific number of rings. There's no way I'm going to remember this is the four seconds of training I receive, so I get busy making tiny stickers for each phone line. Quickly, I see that this is an impossibility, because 3 of these people want their phones picked up after one ring. So if more than one phone line rings at the same time, I'm screwed.

But I'm feeling productive and employable, picking up the phone as best I can on the prescribed number of rings and putting a cheery inflection into my voice. I go through two cans of Diet Coke, jacked on caffeine and feeling like Octopus Lady. There are calls from clients, friends of clients checking to see which editing room they might be in, delivery people and producers anxious for the next cut. Soon there are more calls than any one person with two arms could answer.

I'm aware of a male figure at my side, and pick up the angry energy coming off him. I transfer a call and hang up my extension, turning to him.

"Didn't they say to have my calls picked up on the first ring?"

"I'm sorry, what's your name?"

"Mitchell?" he says, with an irritated air that says I should have known.

I eye my sticky note system and see that yes, he is one of the miracle-seekers asking for something that at some point in every working day, will not be possible. "I do see that, yes."

"Well, is it a problem for you?"

Where to start. "No, it's not a problem, but as you can see, there are a lot of calls, and . . ."

"Good, then I'll be able to get my calls." He stomps off.

Yes, you will. One ring later.

Several others come out of their hidey-holes to yell at me during the day, not seeming to understand that what they're saying is ridiculous. It's not like I'm randomly leaving the desk, or allowing calls to go to voicemail (heaven forbid). It's one more friggin' ring, people. Get over it.

Maybe they're bored and don't know what to do with themselves, or so worried that they're very existence hangs in the balance that one more ring could mean the difference between having a job and being fired. I just keep picking up the receiver, a little more of me draining away each time.

Is this my new life? I have no idea what I'm doing, and miss the camaraderie of the psychic line. I'd rather talk to weirdos who know they're strange than a roomful of supposed important types who think they're normal. I want to learn and grow. I want to fly.

The job lasts one day, but I wouldn't go back there if they paid me.

June
☆ Gemini ☆

I'm on my way.

The sun, which I've been expecting to blaze through my windows each morning slips behind the clouds and Venice is cast into gloom. Since my unfortunate foray into temping, I've been more vigilant about finding work, empowered, I guess, by the notion that maybe I'm not the hugest fuckup in the world. Maybe I do have the skills to be a functioning adult.

I have an interview at a publishing company, and then another. The pay is pathetic, less than half of what I was making in New York, and I realize that when you factor in my per-minute rate, I was making more at the psychic line than I would as an editor. But efforts to negotiate a better hourly rate don't get me much of anywhere, and I'm forced to tell one HR rep that I literally can't live on what they're offering me. She just shrugs her shoulders and goes back to her paperwork.

But I press on. It's been five months since the earthquake and a year for me in Los Angeles. I've been through poverty, a stint at a psychic line and a major tectonic shift. I've lost some friends—don't see much of Opal anymore, and Katie is too busy with her married beau to get together that often—but made others.

Martin is rumored to be looking for investors for a new line, but I have mixed feelings about that. Readers need to make a hell of a lot more to make the wage livable, and that may not be forthcoming anytime soon. I've lost touch with Mercy, Emma, Wilma, but ran into Delia once at the Farmer's Market. Most of my New York friends are toast. The scary black car hasn't made another appearance in my neighborhood. I've committed to this city in a way that feels like a relationship. Maybe if I can start there, the real thing will come along when it's damn good and ready.

My experience with reading cards and charts jumps quickly and I find that the more I do it, the better I can receive information and trust what I get. A few people find their way to me for readings, through friends and flyers I leave around on bulletin boards, and even though it's small, I take it as a sign that I'm meant to continue in this direction. Some are looking for an experience, a performance of clairvoyance like a parlor trick. Others are distraught because of a personal issue and just want comfort. I see an array of humanity I've never touched before, and it completely changes the way I will see the world from this point forward.

In mid-June, Katie calls to ask if I would be interested in doing a party with her, to give readings for guests. It's somewhere in Malibu, up in the hills, and I can just imagine it—recumbent bodies oiled and dripping couture, bored expressions, canned laughter. "I totally appreciate it, Lady, but I'd feel kinda like a clown."

"You love clowns!"

"I have mixed feelings about clowns, but I know I don't want to be one."

"All right, then. I'll get someone else."

Am I wrong to be cavalier about any money that comes my way? I don't know. But a girl's gotta have some self-respect. I try the metaphysical stores around town, now that I have some real experience and a few seasoned names to toss around. But an interview at one goes poorly when I fail to recognize my subject as the reincarnation of Aleister Crowley (my bad) and I hear through the grapevine that another psychic has been robbed outside another, at the end of his shift, when his pockets were filled with cash. Bad rumors circulate about that place, how the owners may have tipped off the thieves. Maybe true, maybe not. But I can't take the chance.

A week later, I hear back from the temp agency about a "long-term" assignment which may last a week or longer. It's testament to my changed perspective that a week actually feels like a long time. She quizzes me about the programs I know, Mac or PC, steno or no. Half of my answers are complete lies. I just want the work.

"This is the vice president of Disney," she says. "You have to have professional clothing and be on your very best behavior. All right?"

"I'll do a good job. Promise."

"That's my girl."

I take down the address and phone number, in case I'm going to be late. I'll figure out the best way to get there from the *Thomas Guide*.

Somehow, I've managed to get a credit card from a chain boutique, so I trek over to the Promenade in Santa Monica to see if I can do some damage and find a professional wardrobe. The saleswoman looks at me like I've landed in the wrong place as I browse through the racks. The last time I can remember shopping in a regular store was over six years ago, when I had to get a dress to wear to a friend's wedding. Even then, I grabbed the first thing that seemed like it might fit, without regard to what I might want to wear in the future. My style, as I see it, is bound up with people who have gone before, and what they have left behind.

I don't even know where to start. Pulling a few tops off a rack, I move to the skirts and then the pants. I'm completely uninspired at the thought of trying to fit in, and having to leave my cool vintage dresses at home. In the dressing room, my worst fears are confirmed as I look at a different person staring back at me. She looks scared, slightly greenish under the lights, and bland. Just like everyone else. I want to run out of there screaming.

But I try on almost everything in the store, willing myself to be mature enough to do this one thing. By then the saleswoman has begun to have a kind of respect for me, perhaps sensing that I will make a large purchase. At least there are a few pieces that aren't entirely hideous, and can go with almost anything. Gray, black, navy—it's all the same, no matter where you live.

When I get home, I just throw the shopping bag on my bed and don't even bother to hang up my new clothes. There's none of that happy-go-lucky feeling behind making a femmy purchase, no breathless excitement to wear them. They're like any other tools—hammers, brushes or brooms—with no real meaning for me. I may never wear them again after this job is finished.

The night before my first day, I can't sleep and lie there staring at the light shifting along the ceiling every time a car goes by. The white noise of the ocean and the shushing of the cars mixes together until all I can think about is shoving as much of my stuff as will fit in a suitcase and just going. I figure I can get as far as Nevada before I run out of gas money, maybe to Texas before I pass out from hunger.

But I get up and go to work, just like any working stiff.

The thing is, I'm not used to driving in rush hour traffic, and have no idea how long it takes to get anywhere at 8:00 in the morning. Venice to Burbank on a good day is maybe forty-five minutes, depending on your route. But today it's more than an hour, and it's lucky that my boss isn't in when I come careening into the office.

It's a small suite in the television department. On the desk blotter are instructions for booting up the computer, and how to answer the phone. This guy doesn't have to have his phone picked up on a certain number of rings, which is lucky. I don't know how much more of that my sanity can stand. The computer password is 1234, no points for originality, and I'm quickly signed on. A picture of a baby dressed up like a flower blooms across the screen and I feel like I've just entered the sixth circle of hell.

But the day passes uneventfully. The boss man comes in and hardly looks at me as he takes his seat in the other room. He gets my name wrong twice, asks me how long I'll be there (the entire week—as long as his regular assistant is on vacation), and acts like making copies is beyond my limited intelligence. I am forbidden to touch the files, which is fine by me. It's clear by the end of the first day that this job is going to entail a lot of magazine reading. Books would be frowned upon, and you can't get that deep into anything when you're answering phones every ten minutes or so.

The worst part is that I have to tell him when I'm going to the bathroom, as if I'm a child on a very short tether. Portraits of Mickey Mouse are spaced at various intervals in the hallway, and there's even one peering from the bathroom door. I scuttle inside, made nervous by his gaze. At the mirror is a woman dressed in a loud floral dress applying frosty pink lipstick. I nod at her and make my way into a stall.

"Are you temping for Laura-Jean?"

I guess she's talking to me. There's no one else here.

"Um, yes. My name is Alyson." Can't say I've ever met anyone on the toilet before. That's a new one for me.

"That's so great. She's a real doll. But tell me, Alyson. Are you free next week? I have to visit my sister in Albuquerque. She's having surgery and I want to be there for her."

With mouth hanging open, I get myself dressed again and join her at the sink. "I'm pretty sure I am," I say. "I have to double check."

Her eyes light up. "Great! That way, I can request you. Mark says you're doing a great job."

He did? Hard to tell if he's even noticed my presence.

I stammer, "That would be great. Thanks a lot."

My hands washed and dried, I shake her hand and make my way out to the hall again. Just for the hell of it, I give Mickey a little wink and a nod. We understand one another now, and I'm part of the club.

By late afternoon, I begin to feel guilty about making twelve bucks an hour for picking up a few phone calls. I look under the desk, but there's so much stuff shoved under there—a space heater, a few boxes of manila envelopes, three pairs of shoes and some subject dividers for notebooks—that I don't want to mess with her personalized system. She may never find anything again. Maybe I can straighten the desk. But it, too, is crammed with figurines from *The Little Mermaid*, *Aladdin* and *The Lion King*, various mugs, pencils and office supplies. I can't even find a Post-It pad to write messages on, or take down the names of people too rushed to make sure you have their numbers. I write them on the cardboard desk blotter instead, and transfer them to some fax paper later, very neatly, to help me fill the rest of the day.

On the weekend, I get together with Katie at my place. With the influx of a little cash, it's not as sad, even though the weather is gloomy again today. By noontime, it will burn off and leave us basking in the sun. Well, me at least. Katie is terrified of wrinkles and slathers herself in SPF 70 if she's driving in the car. So a walk along the boardwalk is going to take several reapplications.

"What do you see in this place?" she asks, when we've cleared the strip of open-front stores selling souvenir t-shirts and not particularly good pizza.

For some reason, I'm not offended. For the first time since I moved here, I feel open and free, believing that those entities I communicated with on the Ouija board really are all around, protecting me. Today it's beautiful and kids are chasing each other on the beach, yelling their little lungs out. What's to worry about?

"I like living by the water." I look over and she's frowning into the tar below. I have to remind myself to not say she'll get wrinkles that way.

"But why here?"

"I don't know. I just feel comfortable with these people. They're on the edge, as far away from New York as possible. They understand what it's like to not quite fit in."

"You mean they're crazy."

"Not crazy, exactly. More like enlightened."

"Enlightened?" Her tone tells me she's scoffing.

"In a literal sense. Enlightened of possessions . . . concerns, money."

This brings a smile to her lips.

"You don't know what you're talking about."

"Maybe not, but I'm trying. And that's something."

The next few weeks rush by so fast, I barely have time to notice that I still live alone and have a long way to go before my life could be considered, uh, settled. The days blur by in a parade of getting up, getting ready, driving to work in thick rush hour traffic and skidding into work, Fred Flintstone style, a few minutes before 9:00.

Some of my jobs last a few hours (4 is the shortest the agency will allow me to work) and some a few weeks or longer. Soon I am able to afford my rent and phone, the utility bills and even some clothing once in awhile. Though most consider temps too stupid to hold down their jobs, most of the temps I meet are sparkling and intelligent, working on theater pieces, art installations and books of short stories. Some are screenwriters in waiting, looking for contacts to send their work to, and some are just undecided, using this time to make some money and figure out exactly what their lives are calling them to do.

When I have a break, I walk around the Walt Disney lot, fascinated by the soundstages at the far end, their enormous sliding doors magnetic and mysterious. Growing up on the East Coast, I have been raised on Disney animation, taught to believe in its fables and moral lessons. As I pass the old animation building, set low to the ground and with drawing tables clearly visible through the casement windows, I vow to sneak in. Luckily, the doors aren't locked, and I trespass shamelessly, peering into each door as if it might contain a trunk filled with untold treasures. On each wall is a series of old cels, from *Sleeping Beauty, Dumbo, Bambi* and *The Sorcerer's Apprentice*. It's like a living museum in the middle of Burbank, and I feel my childhood rise up like it's never done before.

I can picture my smaller self sitting on the floor, my elbows on a turquoise hassock, my hands supporting my chin. A Salisbury steak TV dinner is there, too, waiting to cool down before I can eat it. Then the image of the magic kingdom appears on the television set, its channels still changed by hand, and my attention can't move anywhere else. My food goes cold and gelatinous until I need my knife to pull it away from the sides of the tinfoil container.

You've made it this far, the memory seems to say, *what's a few more steps?*

People spend their lives trying to get this close to the Disney lot. I landed here completely by accident. Maybe there is some luck in the world after all.

I'm in traffic when I realize it's happened. My mind is in that pleasant place between dreaming and wakefulness and I'm watching the sun disappear over the not quite flat line of the earth. The sky is crazy with colors, too many to possibly define. But my mind splats forth a word—*Gemini*—as I steer into the turnoff lane.

Gemini. An Air Sign concerned with all aspects of the mind. People born under this sign need to form ideas, write and express themselves, but also to experience the world around them. Answering the world's most pressing questions remains one of their prime directives. Ruled by Mercury, planet of communication, writing and teaching, these folks can sometimes have a short attention span, but endless curiosity about the world. They're in love with words and may be very verbal in nature, so there may never be enough time to do all they want to do.

Gemini natives make great artists, writers and reporters. They can be so busy, though, that they lose track of their focus or take on more than they can handle. Challenges can arise when they're two-faced, indecisive or unable to commit to one idea, belief or person. They should be careful not to scatter their energies so they don't become run down or sick. Since their symbol is the Twins, they may be a twin, or may feel that they're forever searching for their twin soul, in the form of a mate, mentor or best friend.

The thought runs through my mind as if someone's typing it there. I can actually see the words scrolling past. So many times in the past few months, I've wondered if we're only given one chance at love. I've wondered if mine has passed, left behind in New York as an unsatisfying emotional experiment. But if there's a time to change that belief it's now, when Gemini, sign of second acts, is unfolding in the heavens.

Perhaps the sign of the Twins means that there can be two lovers, or more if they're needed, and a chance to begin again. I look at the road ahead of me, packed bumper to bumper with unhappy people, and see a new path, the road not taken, and the very pavement seems to light up, just a little.

I have not met my future husband yet, but am well on my way to better dating habits. I know what I want and what to avoid like a bad case of botulism. And for the first time in my life, I'm not about to take anything less. In fact, I'm even beginning to like my own company so much that maybe I don't need a partner at all. Maybe I'm so good at this real life stuff that I don't even require my imaginary friends and my endless tarot, astrology and metaphysical books.

OK, let's not get crazy. It's a long life, after all. At least the drive home is a lot easier, and I'm filled with energy when I open the front door that I immediately drop my bag, forego dinner and spend the rest of the night working on my screenplay. The words are flying off my fingers, and it doesn't even seem like I'm writing them anymore. I haven't felt this good in months. I don't even care that in some corners of this fair city, I may seem like the biggest cliché in the world.

On the weekend, I gather up all my books, papers, notes and charts. I stack my dream notebooks up, along with all the channeled material I've done with Katie and Patrice. I've been keeping them scattered around, buried under newspapers and stuffed into my closet with my shoes. The least I can do is bring this part of my life out into the open, to give it the respect it deserves. All of it placed together takes up about five square feet spread out, and stacks to about three feet in height.

Have I really learned this much? I feel like the same person, but in many ways, I'm not. Probably, I won't stop wanting to learn, so why not make a shrine to this seemingly permanent part of my personality? Without another thought, I grab my bag and head out to Ikea. I hear decent shelving units can be found there at a song, for the price of a few hours of your time.

Several hours later, I've become the proud owner of a series of Allen wrenches and a not too shabby bookshelf. I feel like christening it with a bottle of champagne smashed across its shelves. Soon, all my best possessions are lined up and neat. With all this progress, I'm sure to be a grown up one of these days.

The Ouija board occupies a position of honor in this display, but even that needs a bit of a makeover. I need about fifteen minutes to cut out and attach new feet to the planchette, and give the board a quick polish. I'm about to put it back into the box but can't resist a little chat. It's been awhile since I spoke with the entities.

They're in a talkative frame as the planchette flies around. I can feel several spirits entering my body, almost like a bunch of clowns trying to pack a phone booth. In the end I have quite a few pages of new material:

> *You are undergoing an exegesis of sorts, a purging or weeding out. New energies are emblematic of this change. Men represent a part of you that can't decide which way to go. Your head will be turned in many directions, Gemini-like, and it is important for you to keep at least one foot on the ground. You have had much training and much hype along these paths, now it is time to try your wings. Men will be like candy to you soon, delicious but sickening after awhile. See the equation, Einstein? You will succeed when it is time. Meisterworks do not have to come along once or twice in one's career; it is not the one-shot, orgasm blast of creation. That is the man's view of conception, as he provides the sperm. A woman's vision would involve the energy moving from the top of the head downward. That is, from the spiritual in to the womb, the vessel of manifest creation. If you try visualizing with your womb, feel the energy concentrate there and move to whatever chakra is indicated by the desire, you will experience faster and more potent concrete manifestations. Likely chance of a boyfriend soon, but you already knew that. It is one in three now. The others also arrive when you least expect it. Do not discount social obligations or blow off things in the next few weeks. Tiredness is no excuse. Realize that it is also death to be over-prepared, to be "desperately seeking boyfriend." The energy you project now is frightening*

and inviting. It will take a man with some mettle to undo that Gordian knot. You must remain steadfast in your goals and your obligations. Social events will take on a bit of homework-like responsibilities. You are a rock star in a parallel universe. You understand the fatigue of fame, the constant energy sap. Of course, there is the yearning for acclaim, for "love" but it turns out you realize the falseness of such a claim. You're practically there, and just have to work out some details.

When I read it out loud, I have to laugh. After all, it's been about two days since I vowed to respect my own company, to live without the comfort of a mate in my life. Sex is one thing, and love another, right? But perhaps, as my skybound friends are suggesting, both are equally possible. Until I know better, I'll leave both doors open and see who walks through them.

My days in Venice are waning as the romantic allure of this place wears off. Every time summer comes around, I find someone parked in my spot seemingly every weekend, despite the plethora of mean signs rightly claiming that we tow. Sighing, I go inside to drop a dime. They'll find their car someday.

Lately, I've been thinking about Hollywood. If I'm working at Disney, it's a fraction of the commute, and hey, it's what brought me here in the first place. On my days off, I drive up and down some of the less traveled streets there, winding into the hills. The cars seem to cling to the sides of the road, as do the homes themselves. But there's something about being this high up that gives you a completely different view of Los Angeles. Far from the strip mall-marred landscape it seems to visitors, it's now the oasis I'm convinced the first settlers saw when they built their pueblos here. Brought west by the promise of water, they stayed for the weather, the ease of life and then the entertainment business. From this perspective, that seems mildly possible now.

I'm walking up Beachwood Canyon toward the Hollywood sign one day and dreaming about nothing in particular. The sign stands out in stark relief as the sun begins its daily descent, symbol to millions around the globe and site of a few suicides. I have no idea if I'll reach it if I keep walking, but I bend my knees, taking the inclines with the strongest part of my legs. I put my head down and doggedly make my way upward, letting my senses reach out to explore the brilliant bougainvillea, the sharp staccato of parrots overhead.

Then I become aware of a car to my right. It's a tourist couple, obvious by the map spread wide across their laps. I pull part of my headset away from my ears.

"Do you know how to get to the Hollywood sign?" the man asks, in a thick German accent.

"I . . . uh . . . well, I'm headed up there myself."

"So you know the way to go?"

"I . . ." *Do I, really?*

"I don't think you can get here by car," I say. "But on foot, you may have a chance."

They thank me, accelerate and make their way north. I keep walking, determined now to see if I can get there. Maybe it will mean something, maybe not. But I have to try.

Ten minutes later, another car stops me, and then another. Truthfully, I don't know how to get to the Hollywood sign. It's all the way up that hill, and since more than a few people have jumped to their death from it, they've made it hard to get to for a reason. But after I explain to the fourth carload of anxious tourists that they should just drive north, then turn at the stop sign, they're happy to comply.

What have they seen, I wonder? Someone who seems like they know where they're going? If so, maybe there's hope for me in this toughest of towns.

By some miracle occurrence, I begin to get to work five minutes early, then ten. I don't want to push it, but having the time to walk instead of run to the office feels pretty good. It's Thursday, not quite the weekend, and I'm happy or merely caffeinated as I take my desk. Reading over the instructions—there are always instructions—I turn on the computer and crack open a diet soda (some habits don't break that easily). When I toss my bag on the desk, some stuff spills out, and I'm not even thinking about it until one of my co-workers is standing there.

"Are those tarot cards?"

I've successfully hidden my weirdo tendencies from these seemingly normal folks for a few weeks now, intent on being a decent enough citizen to pay my bills and achieve some self-sufficiency along the way. And for a moment, my brain seizes, unable to decide whether it's better to tell the truth and possibly out myself as a gypsy witch who can't be trusted, or deny it to the hilt.

I think I can get another temp job. "Yeah," I say.

"You read cards?" The excitement in her voice is unmistakable.

What to say, what to say.

"I'm . . . well, yes. I learned in college."

"I've always wanted to learn how to read cards."

Please don't ask me to teach you.

261

"Do you think you could give me a reading? Is that all right?"

The computer's finished booting, and the instructions have been read. "Sure, just let me take these messages off the voicemail and we can get started."

"Yay! I'll get my coffee and be right back!"

I don't know if she's my new best friend, or someone I'll be avoiding in a few hours. But it's happening, at Disney, right now. I write down three phone messages and arrange them next to the mail, for whenever today's boss arrives.

The girl comes back a few minutes later, bearing a cup of coffee for me, too, which I have to refuse. "My name's Gerry, by the way. Sorry to bust in on you like this, but I don't know anyone else who reads cards at Disney."

"I'm Alyson," I say. "It's no problem, but we'll probably have to keep it to one spread, in case any one comes by, all right?"

She shuffles the cards, cuts them into three piles to the left and looks at me. I gather them up and lay out a quick Celtic Cross, seeing immediately that she's worried about a love relationship. A "should I stay or should I go" situation.

"It's not as bad as you think," I begin, then stop. "You wanted to ask about a guy, right?'

"How did you know that?"

"I can just see it."

"So he's . . ."

"There are other people around him, and sometimes women, but he's interested in learning more about you, getting to know you, and certainly likes you a lot."

"Really?" Her energy practically melts all over the chair. And I'm not lying to preserve her feelings. It's just so clear to me, the images so present, that I couldn't possibly *not* see them, even if I tried.

"He really likes you. You don't need to stress about it. I know it's normal to worry, but as of this moment in time, he's here for you. I know you're not asking me what I would do . . ."

"But what *would* you do?" She's so earnest then that I laugh, liking her right away.

"I would stay, and learn about him. Develop my own life somehow, with friends, hobbies or both. Find my own path and hope that his dovetailed with mine somehow." The words come out of my mouth so quickly that it almost doesn't seem like I've said them.

When did I become an expert in romance?

But she's so grateful, she stops by my desk on her way to the commissary at lunchtime. "I was wondering if you had any lunch plans. Maybe I can get you a sandwich or something for the reading?"

I haven't been there yet, so I'm happy to accept. "That's not necessary, but thanks for offering. I definitely appreciate it."

We walk out of the building into the warm sun and it's one of those days that you're not only happy to be alive, but to be human and mostly devoid of suffering on this spinning blue planet. The birds are tweeting like a bunch of *Snow White* extras and even the shrubbery is clipped into Mickey's shape as we make our way into the obviously vintage cafeteria. It's lined with photos of old time movie stars, Walt himself and even a smattering of contemporary actors. I'm staring like an open-mouthed fool and Gerry has to pull me along by the strap of my purse into the line for sandwiches. There are so many choices I can't make up my mind, and for a few minutes I have to concentrate on my breathing so it won't run away from me, my heart leaping from my chest like a cartoon character and splashing into the condiments.

We get our stuff—turkey sandwich on rye with cranberry sauce for me and grilled Swiss on wheat for her—and walk toward a series of tables. Gerry turns to me, "I see some people from features over there. Let's join them, OK?"

It's getting loud in here, so I nod my assent and follow behind. We end up in the far right corner of the room, at a large table of rowdy, debating twenty—and thirty-somethings. A tall guy with softly waved brown hair and eyes to match gets up when he sees Gerry trying to pull an extra chair over for me. When our eyes meet, I feel an electric little thrill move down my spine. But it's too early for things like that, I tell myself. Not the right time or place.

"Gerry, who's your friend?"

"Hey, Ben, this is Alyson. She's working with us in TV."

I extend my hand and he shakes it with a grin. "So what brings you to this place?"

I realize I'm pressed in next to him and suppose I'm lucky not to have a six-foot boner poking out of my pants. Whatever the female equivalent is, I have that. Totally.

"Uh, the 134, I guess?" I'm not even trying to be funny, but he cracks up, looking at Gerry.

"I can tell I'm going to like you," he says, and we don't stop talking the rest of the time we're eating. I'm hoping Gerry doesn't think I'm ignoring her, after her kind insistence on paying for the sandwiches and just because it's not a cool thing to do.

But when we rise to empty our trays into the garbage and go back to work, Ben follows us.

"Nice to have met you."

"Isn't she cool?" Gerry asks.

We're looking at each other and I don't know about him but I'm pretty much oblivious to whatever else is going on around me.

"She is indeed. Maybe I'll stop by and visit you later."

"Sounds good," I say, not trusting my voice with any additional syllables.

He pulls at the door and the sun streams in, lighting up his hair like a halo. He holds it open.

A door opens, you gotta walk through it.

The rest is up to the universe.

Epilogue

Though Ben and I had a really fun time, and dated briefly, we didn't end up together. The last time I heard anything about him, he was married to a woman who also works at Disney, and had two very cute kids with his huge brown eyes.

It would be six years before I met my future husband, a member of the same online writing workshop I attended from time to time. He was living in Sacramento when we met; I was in Los Angeles. It was in Burbank Airport, seeing him off after our first weekend together that I realized I'd seen this all before. Kissing him at the gate, I had a flash of a dream I'd had, of being in an airport and trying to be brave as my lover left. I remembered crying a little and him hugging me to his chest. But most of all it was the feeling inside me, as if a million butterflies had just been released in my heart. That feeling didn't go away until he moved down to be with me. We married a few years later. Later, I found out he had wed his first wife on the day I left New York for Los Angeles, a woman with the same initials as me.

A few years after we met, I was able to claim my gift and begin calling myself a "real" psychic, though I prefer the term "intuitive healer." These days, I'm married, happy, and have a very successful practice as the Sassy Psychic (http://www.sassypsychic.com). On a daily basis, I get to help people all over the world, and I love my job.

I've lost touch with my former compatriots, but still think of them fondly. And to this day, I don't know whether that long black car was government issued or not. With the passage of time, I'm grateful for the experience of the psychic line, not angry about having to survive on less than a person can. My co-workers were truly gifted, deserving of both admiration and fair treatment. So the next time you're looking for a psychic reading, think about what you might be making possible in their lives with your money. Many of them attend classes, workshops and seminars to keep their skills sharp for you. Their pay should be commensurate with their abilities.

Our fascination with other worlds, with spirits and messages from the other side, isn't likely to go away anytime soon. Feed a psychic or, better yet, develop your own intuition. Someday, it may help you make decisions, cope with difficulty and yes, even manifest a new relationship. My hopes are with you there.

Acknowledgments

I'd like to thank early readers and supporters of *Searching for Sassy*, as well as fellow psychics, intuitive healers, and energy workers around the world. You are the light, my friends.

Deep bow of appreciation to my clients, who continue to inspire me, and keep my heart dancing.

I am indebted to my teachers, too numerous to list individually. From musicians and artists to writers, thinkers, creators, adventurers and weirdos, you have all fed me, and I thank you.

And to NB, you rule in all possible ways.

About the Author

Psychic since childhood, Alyson Mead been reading people since the age of 19, and developing her natural abilities with certifications at the highest levels in astrology, tarot, Reiki, Matrix Energetics, Neuro-Linguistic Programming, Mindfulness-Based Stress Reduction, dream interpretation, and sound healing. She is the bestselling author of *Wake Up to Your Stories* and *Wake Up to Your Weight Loss,* and her fiction, essays and articles have appeared in over thirty publications. Alyson has also received the Columbine Award for Screenwriting, the Roy W. Dean Filmmaking Grant, and awards from *Writer's Digest* and *USA Book News.* She's internationally known as the Sassy Psychic (http://www.sassypsychic.com), and loves helping people all over the world.